PALE CREAM

Sir Edward Elgar (1857-1934)
COMPOSER

Fortified British Wine
Selected by Tesco

75 cl e

15% vol

The Master Musicians Series

ELGAR

Series edited by Stanley Sadie

TO

MY WIFE, ELIZABETH

PREFACE

ON THE factual side of Elgar's life the present volume must to a large extent be a summary, as many books are available on the subject. The most valuable early sources are Buckley and Newman, whilst in 1955 appeared the treatments by Dr Percy Young, detailed and thorough, and Miss Diana McVeagh, discerning and imaginative. Dr Young followed up his biography with two valuable collections of letters. Michael Kennedy's *Portrait of Elgar* (1968) sees the composer in yet another light.

Then there are my own views when it comes to assessing the major compositions: these are unaffected by personal friendships and so can be contrasted with those of biographers such as Reed and Maine. I have been able to approach the personalities 'pictured within' the *Enigma Variations* without being tied to existing opinions, which had tended to solidify. I did in fact once meet Troyte Griffith—and was able to confirm the suspicion of others that he was unlike his apparent musical portrait—but, by and large, I live in a post-Elgarian world and know the composer only through his music, through memories of others and, to a fair extent, through visiting many parts of Worcestershire and the cottage, Brinkwells, in Sussex.

The two chapters on the *Enigma variations* contain entirely new material, as does the study in Chapter XII of the sketches of the slow movement of Symphony No. 2. I am indebted to the Right Reverend John Richards, the Lord Bishop of St Davids, who helped me to solve the first part of the enigma, and to Mr Alan Webb, curator of the Birthplace, who has been untiring with his assistance in every possible way.

I am grateful also to Mrs Joyce Crook, Miss Winifred Barrows and Mr A. T. Shaw for much practical help, and to Dr Percy Young for encouragement. For permission to use photographs I am grateful to Mrs Iliffe (Dr Sinclair and Dan), Mr E. A. Butcher

('Dorabella') and to Messrs Alan Meek and Desmond Tripp, E.M.I. and the B.B.C. My warm thanks to Dr David Harries for preparing the Index. Finally I am particularly grateful to the late Mrs Elgar Blake, not only for permission to reproduce her father's music and to quote from her mother's diary, but also for the friendly personal interest she took in my work.

IAN PARROTT

Aberystwyth.
1971

NOTE ON THE SECOND IMPRESSION

Two important books have appeared since this was first published: *Edward Elgar. The Record of a Friendship* by Rosa Burley and Frank L. Caruthers (Barrie & Jenkins, 1972), and *Elgar. A Life in Photographs* by Jerrold N. Moore (O.U.P., 1972). My continued research on the Enigma can be followed in 'Elgar's Two-Fold Enigma: a Religious Sequel' in *Music & Letters* (Vol. 54, No. 1, January 1973), and a discerning article, which I had previously not seen, is 'Elgar's Last Judgment' by Arnold Whittall in *The Music Review* (Vol. 26, No. 1, February 1965). There is also 'Delius & Elgar: A Postscript' by Rachel Lowe-Dugmore in *Studies in Music*, No. 8, 1974 (Perth, W. Australia).

Rosa Burley confirms many of our suspicions about Elgar's character and also my deductions which led, I think, to the solving of the enigma. She saw much of Elgar in the autumn of 1898 and the 'supposed enigmatical significance was not, I think, mentioned at that time'; the piano rolls notes 'differ in some details from what he told me in 1898 and in one case in even the identity of the person concerned'. Lady Mary Lygon, she says, was not in fact the original of Variation No. 13. On the other characters she is quite discerning, though Miss Burley unfortunately swallows the dog story for G.R.S. without question. On my other part of the solution, she confirms in two different places that Elgar had a 'very good knowledge of' and an 'immense interest in' the Protestant Bible. She also confirms that he who had 'never been near the Iberian Peninsula', could catch 'the evening atmosphere of its towns' (in *Spanish Serenade*).

I have looked at several more versions of the 'enigma' line in St Paul. Tyndale, 1534, says 'Now we se in a glasse even in a darke speakynge' and Luther's bible (Tübingen, 1767) gives, 'Wir sehen jetzt durch einem spiegel in einem dunckeln worte'. Both confirm Elgar's 'dark saying'. Another retired bishop has come to my aid on the other problem. The Rt Rev. L. M. Charles-Edwards says he does not think bulldogs are fond of water. Unlike retrievers or labradors they would not, he says, leap into a river to recover sticks thrown by even a beloved Master. Which is confusing, since Sir Ivor Atkins used to discuss with Elgar the point at which Dan fell into the Wye. Perhaps he slipped.

I. P.

Aberystwyth, 1977

MUSIC ACKNOWLEDGMENTS

THE extracts from Elgar's works are quoted by permission of the publishers:

Messrs Novello & Co. Ltd, for *The Dream of Gerontius*, *Enigma Variations*, *Falstaff*, *King Olaf*, *Introduction and Allegro*, *The Kingdom*, *The Wand of Youth*, *Chanson de Matin*, Symphony No. 1, Symphony No. 2, Violoncello Concerto and String Quartet.

Messrs Boosey & Hawkes Music Publishers Ltd, for *Coronation Ode*, *Sea Pictures* and *Pomp & Circumstance* marches.

The extract from the Organ Sonata is reproduced by permission of British & Continental Music Agencies Ltd, London.

The quotation from Walton's *Belshazzar's Feast* is used by permission of the Oxford University Press and that from Puccini's *Manon Lescaut* by permission of Messrs G. Ricordi & Co. (London), Ltd.

CONTENTS

ILLUSTRATIONS

Between pages 52 and 53

CHAPTER I

THE SETTING: THE SALON

IN THE Soviet Union there is a birthplace museum proudly com-
memorating Tchaikovsky; in Italy they pay similar homage to
Verdi; and in the Germanic countries the habit had already been
formed, so that the 'Beethovenhaus' at Bonn is only one of many
composer museums. In Britain after the seventeenth century no
such custom prevailed. The domination of the German foreigners,
first Handel and then Mendelssohn, was accepted without
question; there seemed to be no native-born composers of standing
in this country, and thus the art of enjoying any relics or associations died out.

By the second half of the nineteenth century Great Britain was
well on the way to commanding the largest empire the world had
ever known and national pride was at its most buoyant. The class
structure, however, had its rigid divisions and all professional
musicians, performers, teachers and creators alike, were expected
to belong if not to the company of 'rogues and vagabonds' at least
to the lowest stratum. In fact they were looked upon as unlikely
and unwelcome amongst the higher strata, the tradespeople and
the landed gentry, who were happy to be amateur performers for
light amusement only and for whom *salon* music was adequate.
The only exception for a British professional musician was to be
associated with the hierarchy of the Church, which then, very
much more than now, occupied a central position in every com-
munity. The use of the word 'imperial', not only for colleges and
museums but also for hotels, was natural in those expansive times.
Foreign musicians, who were looked down upon, could come
from anywhere and frequently the best came from Germany. As
there were in fact very few British-born composers of real worth,
this attitude of mind not unnaturally hardened and it has been a

long time—about a hundred years—before any change has come about in the general public's mind.

About three miles west of Worcester on the Bromyard road there is something which is still unique in Britain: a signpost pointing the way to a composer's birthplace. Along the side lane in the direction of the signpost there is a cottage half a mile short of the village of Broadheath. Here Edward William Elgar was born on 2nd June 1857. More than thirty years after his death this cottage has become the symbol of a great composer: it is a birthplace museum.

Another, if negative, sign of the slow recognition of genius has been his changing image. All his life and for many years afterwards Elgar was thought of as the musical embodiment of imperialism, a jingo who looked like a cross between a squire and a colonel. Gradually the image has changed as the true facts have come more and more to light, so that by 1968 a *Portrait*[1] shows him as a neurotic, withdrawn dreamer, cut off and infinitely sad. 'He encountered snobbery, both social and artistic, and it wounded him,' says Michael Kennedy. 'Somewhere . . . something or someone wounded him so deeply, so irreparably, that he never fully recovered . . . he buried the secret of this wound in his heart. It showed itself only in the anguish and solitude of certain passages in his music.'

Edward Elgar was the second son of William Henry Elgar and Anne Greening. Much detailed information on both families is given in the opening chapter of Dr Percy M. Young's *Elgar O.M.* Elgar's father was organist of St George's Roman Catholic Church in Worcester and also kept a music shop. When the family was growing the Elgars moved out to the quieter countryside of Broadheath, but a few years later, when Edward was between two and three, they moved back into Worcester again. What the city could offer the growing boy was the organ loft, the music and books in the shop and provincial concerts. His father had introduced him to the music of Bach by the age of nine; the boy had concocted an anagram on the name—he had inherited an interest in history and literature from his mother. Some of his first tunes, later a basis for

[1] Michael Kennedy, *Portrait of Elgar* (1968), pp. 3 and 271.

the *Wand of Youth* suites, were written in his early teens.[1] At this time also he was amused by the contradictory statements on the 'rules' of various music theorists.[2]

The Victorian world in which he grew up was rich, confident and stable, but indifferent to artistic values. This became increasingly irksome for a man who, self-taught, knew he had more to offer than was dreamed of around him; contemporary indifference made him more bitter than if he had had to contend with the political upheavals and the constantly divided loyalties that most European composers of stature had had as both burden and stimulus.

Elgar never lived under the shadow of the atom bomb. He acquired considerable skill in science and later conducted his own private experiments, but he would have shared the view of Rutherford: that the splitting of the atom could have no practical application. Nor did he live in the days of experiment as a substitute for creativity.

His schooldays, during which he learnt the violin, were nevertheless happy, almost happy-go-lucky, and he enjoyed pranks and jokes as much as anyone.[3] His apprenticeship to a solicitor in 1872 lasted for only a year, after which he turned wholly to music, helping his father at the organ, in the shop and as violinist and conductor of the Worcester Glee Club. By 1877 he could afford to go to London for a few violin lessons. 'Do you compose?' asked Adolphe Pollitzer, his teacher. 'I try,' Elgar replied. Some of his earliest works, music for the Roman Catholic service, date from this time; he also played the violin in the important (Anglican) Festival of the Three Choirs of Hereford, Gloucester and Worcester when it took place in Worcester in 1878. His considerable feeling for orchestral instruments grew also from playing the bassoon in a wind quintet in which his brother Frank played the oboe. The next year his appointment as band instructor of the Powick lunatic asylum gave him teaching, coaching and, even

[1] Percy Young, *Elgar O.M.* (1955), pp. 31, 35 and 37.
[2] W. H. Reed, *Elgar* (1939), p. 6; R. J. Buckley, *Sir Edward Elgar* (1905), pp. 11–13.
[3] Diana M. McVeagh, *Edward Elgar* (1955), p. 5.

more important, composing experience. More like a painter than a composer, he wrote part of a symphony, bar by bar, on the framework of Mozart's G minor and considered that it was a very useful discipline.

Visits to both Paris and Leipzig at this time were rewarding, though he did not show the same precocious talent that his fellow-countryman, Sullivan, had displayed in the latter town a quarter of a century earlier. Leipzig gave both composers one lasting influence which was to be fundamental: Schumann. Though Sullivan lost it in a welter of trivialities in his declining years, Elgar, in his 'third' period during and after World War I, was to display this influence in a new and refined light. At this time Elgar also followed Sullivan at the Crystal Palace, with the encouragement of August Manns, but his modest *Sevillaña* lacked the brilliance of the *Tempest* music of the older composer. It was a *salon* piece by a 'provincial' with talent, and the first piece of his to be performed in London.

More pieces were written, some were performed and a few were actually published. Perhaps the most successful of his *salon* pieces was *Salut d'Amour*, written in 1888. Messrs Schott & Co. soon changed the German *Liebesgruss* to the more lucrative French title [1] and by giving the composer the name Ed. Elgar they left his nationality in doubt, much as Simrock had done deliberately with Ant. Dvořák. 1889 was the year of Elgar's marriage to Caroline Alice Roberts, one of his pupils. The daughter of the late Major-General Sir Henry Gee Roberts was thought by her family to have 'married beneath her', according to the strict class code of the time, but she was the right person to help this particular composer on the hard road to recognition—and she had a small income. One of the wedding presents was a copy of *The Dream of Gerontius* by Cardinal Newman, with annotations made by General Gordon,[2] a national hero whom Elgar wished to commemorate in music, though the project was never completed.

[1] Kennedy, *op. cit.,* p. 27.
[2] It was not, however, the copy he had in Khartoum before being killed in 1884 (Young, *op. cit.,* pp. 61 and 336).

CHAPTER II

SLOW RECOGNITION: THE CATHEDRAL

NEWLY married, the Elgars settled in London for a while, but in spite of the extra help of a devoted wife the music made little head-way with publishers or concert promoters, though the concert overture *Froissart* was performed at the Worcester Festival and pub-lished in 1890, the year in which their only child, Carice, was born. The important *Serenade* for strings was completed early in 1892. In 1891 they had settled under the massive hills of Malvern and Elgar had to take up again some of the teaching and playing which he had hoped to be rid of for good.

Mrs Norah Parker of Hereford makes it quite clear how Elgar hated teaching. As a scared young girl, she learned the violin from him between 1894 and 1897. He played the piano the whole time, eyed the golf clubs in the corner and showed that 'teaching dread-ful children was the most loathsome thing in life', she wrote.

Between 1842 and 1872 Malvern had been a famous spa under Dr James Wilson and Dr James Manby Gully;[1] in 1876 the latter was involved in the famous Bravo murder mystery (see 'Poison at the Priory' by Elizabeth Jenkins, the *Sunday Times* magazine, 20th October 1968). Elgar was often to be afflicted with headaches and colds but, strangely, he preferred to take the waters at Llandrindod. More visits to Germany meant hearing more music, including a considerable amount of Wagner, another lasting influence on his style. He wrote 'TRISTAN' in capital letters in his diary.[2] The *Tannhäuser* march was first introduced to the Three Choirs Festival in 1883[3] and Elgar arranged it for piano the same year; similarly the *Parsifal* prelude appeared in Hereford Cathedral

[1] Vincent Waite, *Malvern Country* (1968), pp. 29–43.

[2] Reed, *op. cit.*, p. 36.

[3] Watkins Shaw, *The Three Choirs Festival* (Worcester, 1954).

for the first time in 1891 and a few years later Elgar arranged the Good Friday music for small orchestra. The compositions which followed, however, were not operas: they were cantatas. *The Black Knight* (1893), *From the Bavarian Highlands* (1896) and *The Light of Life* (1896) were given at Worcester, while *King Olaf* was performed at the North Staffordshire Festival, also in 1896. It was creatively a very fertile and vigorous period in Elgar's development, and in this 'splendid Saga-ing' (Alice's note on *King Olaf*) there was also the influence of Sullivan's best cantata, *The Golden Legend*, written for the Leeds Festival of 1886, and of Dvořák, whose cantata *The Spectre's Bride* was first given in Birmingham in 1885.

Elgar made many friends, mostly living in or near to Malvern, and some of them were soon to be immortalized in the first truly great work, the *Enigma Variations*. One who did not live locally was August Johannes Jaeger, a German who was a music assistant and eventually a reader at Novello's. He was a true friend and supporter who had much faith in the young composer. In fact it was the German in him that appreciated the real worth of Elgar, who was neither a purveyor of anthems and ballads nor a cathedral organist nor a director of music in a college for boys.[1] Elgar hated more than anything being lumped with these 'mechanical' composers. 'Many a young composer,' said Vaughan Williams, 'has stifled his natural impulses in the desire to be musicianly' [2]—by which he also meant 'mechanical'.

Another good friend was Dr G. R. Sinclair, who gave a performance of the first movement of the year-old Organ Sonata at Hereford Cathedral in December 1896. Of a fugue in *The Light of Life* Elgar told Buckley:[3] 'I thought a fugue would be expected of me. The great British public would hardly tolerate oratorio without fugue ... in short there's enough counterpoint to give the real British religious respectability.' But then turning suddenly serious, as was his way: 'Bach has done it. No man has

[1] See Percy Young (ed.), *Letters to Nimrod* (1965), p. 3.
[2] R. Vaughan Williams, *The Vocalist*, May 1902.
[3] Buckey, R. J., *Sir Edward Elgar* (1905), p. 31.

a greater reverence for Bach than I . . . [but] I don't write in the Bach style.' Then, after saying that the old theorists were not entitled to lay down hard and fast rules for all composers to the end of time, he walked out into the garden of Forli and continued: 'There is music in the air, music all around us, the world is full of it and [here he raised his hands and made a rapid gesture of capture] and—you—simply—take as much as you require!' He was both inspired and eclectic at this time. He would listen with grave and courteous attention to skilled comment on his work but was inclined to make patronizing or incompetent critics wish that they had never opened their mouths.

Travel at the time was mainly by various horse-drawn vehicles. If you read Winifred Norbury's diary for 3rd May 1897 you will see that 'Lady Mary Lygon called on horseback'. Bicycles were also used extensively: Dora Penny (Dorabella) thought nothing of the forty miles from Wolverhampton in 1899.[1] And there was much slogging on foot.

A certain amount of material success and eventual promotion followed some 'occasional' music: the *Imperial March* and *The Banner of St George*, both performed in 1897. Then Elgar's mother got him interested in the story of the British chieftain who defied the Romans, and thus *Caractacus* was conceived. In the spring of the next year the Elgars took over Birchwood Lodge in the country (at the opposite end of the Malvern range to Alice's old home, Redmarley) and there he finished *Caractacus*, which was dedicated to the Queen and performed at the Leeds Festival in the autumn. Elgar's patriotic outlook, as shown in these works, was perfectly natural in an Englishman of the time, as was also a reticent lack of showiness, because 'we are too strong to need it' (see his letter to Jaeger of 5th November 1899). There was much of the typical countryman's outdoor life too, ranging from bicycling and kite-flying to beagling and fox-hunting. Birchwood adjoins the Norbury estate and Winifred Norbury (soon to be in the

[1] Mrs Richard Powell, *Edward Elgar. Memories of a Variation* (2nd ed., 1947), p. 17.

Enigma Variations) helped with the copying of the parts. 'Do *not* trouble,' he wrote on 10th September 1898, 'if you are at all

1 busy
2 tired
3 ill
4 lazy
5 unwilling.'

A very typical letter. Lifting her long Victorian dress above her brightly buttoned boots, Winifred would sometimes show her elegant ankles—quite a bold move in those prim days. In February 1899 Lady Mary Lygon and she came to tea when Elgar had just finished his *Variations*. The next month the Elgars moved to Craeg Lea at Malvern Wells nearer 'Caractacus' hill, and in June Richter conducted the new work at St James's Hall, London. The most important period of Elgar's creativity had arrived when he was already in his forties. He is known still in every corner of the globe, even by the most 'insular' of nations, by the *Enigma Variations*, Op. 36, if by nothing else. Dedicated to his friends 'pictured within', the work's enigma was never disclosed (for a discussion see Chapter VIII). W. H. Reed, one of his closest friends, thought that it was probably a joke,[1] and Diana McVeagh pertinently remarks that 'Elgar, who, when the work came out, seemed almost to want his secret to be guessed . . . in later years replied to questions about it with answers as enigmatical as the enigma'.[2] What was not fully realized at the time was that the orchestration was masterly far beyond anything that had come out of England.

After *Sea Pictures* (one with words by Alice), his active mind soon became engaged in one of his greatest religious compositions: *The Dream of Gerontius*. This tremendously personal setting of Cardinal Newman's poem was finished early in 1900 and the full score completed in August. The performance at Birmingham in October was not a great success. Stanford was reported to have

[1] *Op. cit.*, p. 53.
[2] *Op. cit.*, p. 26.

said: 'My boy, it stinks of incense'—a dig at Elgar's Catholic convictions rather than at the musical style of the work. However, he
did arrange for Elgar to receive an honorary doctorate of Cambridge University, where he himself was Professor of Music. Later
Elgar, the English Catholic, and Stanford, the Irish Protestant, did
not get on so well.

In retrospect we can see the Wagnerian influences which had
been quietly accumulating, so that the use of leading motives is
understandable—though Elgar himself said he got this idea from
Mendelssohn's *Elijah*.[1] The Wagner cult was spreading: such
books appeared as Freda Winworth's *The Epic of Sounds: An
Elementary Interpretation of Wagner's Nibelungen Ring* (1898), and
others were to follow on the 'ethics' and the 'symbolism' and
many other aspects since lost sight of. Strange though the continental musical language of *Gerontius* might have been to the
average English musician, there was a chance that a sympathetic
hearing might be found for it in Germany. And so it turned out.
Jaeger saw it as a second *Parsifal* [2] and got in touch with Julius
Buths, in whose German translation it was performed at the
Lower Rhine Festival at Düsseldorf in December 1901. When
the work was repeated in May the following year Richard Strauss
referred to Elgar as the first English progressive musician. Strauss's
very different treatment of a similar theme, *Tod und Verklärung*, had
been given in England for the first time in 1897. *Gerontius* waited
a further two years before being accepted for a full performance in
its native land. Some popular works were written, however: the
first two *Pomp and Circumstance* marches and the overture *Cockaigne*
(London Town). Of the trio to the first march King Edward VII
is said to have remarked: 'You have composed a tune which will
go round the world.' With the words 'Land of Hope and Glory'
added (despite Jaeger's objection: see letter of 6th December 1901)
it has certainly done that. The words were added when it was put
into the *Coronation Ode*, Op. 44 (1902). 'It was no disgrace,' said
Elgar, referring to the time of the troubadours and bards, 'for a

[1] *Musical Times*, October 1900.
[2] McVeagh, *op. cit.*, pp. 29 and 32.

man to be turned on to step in front of an army and inspire them with a song.'[1] He had reached the hearts of the people, as Sir Hugh Allen said later to Hubert Parry—or perhaps Parry said it.[2] There were to be a total of five *Pomp and Circumstance* marches, wherein we do indeed 'hear the Nation march Beneath her ensign as an eagle's wing' (Lord de Tabley).[3]

If the word 'imperial' is in the mind when we contemplate one side of Elgar's nature, so the word 'dream' represents the other. After some incidental music, Op. 42, to *Grania and Diarmid* by Yeats and George Moore, we note a characteristic title for Op. 43, *Dream Children* (inspired by an essay of Lamb). Indeed by the time of *The Music Makers* ten years later one almost suspects that his references to dreamers and dreaming have become an obsession. At the least we are reminded of the introspective lonely artist in a predominantly extrovert world. Even *King Olaf* had stood and dreamed (vocal score, p. 19) to characteristic music. No doubt Michael Kennedy was right to say that Elgar's music was 'at its first peak of popularity when Britain's greatness was uncontested', but to hear it now as 'the funeral march of a civilization . . . which was decaying' is being somewhat wise after the event.[4] Purcell also transcended his age and there was plenty of 'Rule, Britannia' to come.

Elgar's mother died in September 1902. Within ten days he had the solemn satisfaction of conducting *The Dream of Gerontius* in its entirety in the Three Choirs Festival at Worcester, where his subtly blended scoring had the benefit of the fine acoustics of the Cathedral.[5] He was now thoroughly in the mood for a truly biblical oratorio and had already started to compile the text for *The Apostles*, on which he worked during most of the following year. The majestic reverberation of a great cathedral is even more part of

[1] *Strand Magazine*, May, 1904.

[2] McVeagh, *op. cit.*, p. 55.

[3] Ernest Newman, *Elgar* (1904), p. 150.

[4] *Op. cit.*, p. 151.

[5] For a full account of the early performances of *Gerontius* see Kennedy, *op. cit.*, pp. 86–108.

the designed orchestration and, as *Gerontius* was a nineteenth-century work, so the new oratorio looks forward stylistically to the twentieth. The very opening bars, *Lento* and *solenne*, anticipate the style of Vaughan Williams, while the unrelated root position chords ('Christ's Prayer') of the second section, 'In the Mountain —Night', do so even more. There are still the echoes of Wagner and Franck—'render therefore unto César the things that are Franck's,' said one wag—and other composers, but here is Elgar's most mature and individual language in all its richness and with an unmistakable personality. He did not of course write specifically to a commission. As he himself said: [1] 'A composer worthy the name never waits for an order before setting to work. He is always thinking out works, always making sketches.' Indeed the idea of writing about the apostles dated back to his schooldays.

After the first performance at the Birmingham Festival in October 1903, Myles B. Foster wrote that Elgar 'appears to have shaken off all models and become a law and idiom to himself'.[2] It is doubtful, even so, if Foster had more than an inkling of the significance of the 'mosaic' building of material—for example, one page of 'In the Mountain' contains five separate elements, or 'motives', which can occur later in the oratorio in any different order. After all, it has taken people more than fifty years to appreciate this method of construction in Debussy, whose *La Mer* was written at this time. While Debussy was considered as hopelessly incomprehensible, Elgar was being judged by post-Beethoven sonata-form criteria. As he advanced, therefore, he met new forms of incomprehension, and he was influenced by Brahms usually only when at his worst. There are now no long, gay, sweeping scherzo movements like the last of the *Bavarian Highlands* or many parts of *King Olaf*. Yet after the ancient Jewish shofar has heralded the morning psalm and before the laconic statement 'and when it was day, He called unto Him His disciples', there is such a sunrise for orchestra alone as only Elgar could write. This again combines various elements—even a suggestion of Brahms—and makes

[1] See Buckley, *op. cit.*, p. 73.
[2] Reed, *op. cit.*, p. 72.

shattering use of the three chords representing Christ, the Man of Sorrows, in the texture of those unrelated chords.

Ex.1
'Christ, the Man of Sorrows'

Not even the dawn of Debussy's *La Mer*, finished at Eastbourne in 1905, is more orchestrally colourful. Elgar was original also in his libretto, particularly when he took the view that Judas wished only to force Christ to display his miraculous powers to save himself from death. Buckley [1] was perspicacious enough to consider this work an advance on *Gerontius* in technique, conception and originality of invention. Later commentators have not followed him, because mostly they have been mesmerized by the traditional 'unity' of the earlier work.

[1] *Op. cit.*, p. 79.

CHAPTER III

MATURITY: THE CONCERT HALL

ELGAR had now 'arrived'. An all-Elgar festival at Covent Garden took place in 1904, which included the new exuberant overture *In the South*, written after a visit to Alassio in Italy. In July he was knighted and the Elgars moved once more, this time further west to a house outside Hereford named Plas Gwyn. Elgar was further honoured in many ways both at home and abroad, including a doctorate at Oxford University. Still not wealthy, he reluctantly accepted the Peyton Professorship of Music at Birmingham University, but was glad to hand over to Bantock after he had given a series of controversial lectures during two sessions (he resigned formally in August 1908). He had had misgivings and some ill-health throughout, but still had compositions to occupy him, the most important being the *Introduction and Allegro* for strings, which was finished early in 1905. Despite his military appearance, says Diana McVeagh,[1] his physique was by no means robust and he did not enjoy travelling, although it became increasingly necessary. In June he went with Lady Elgar to America (one of several visits) where he received an honorary degree from Yale University and formed a friendship with the Professor of Music, S. S. Sanford.

The second subject of the sonorous *Introduction and Allegro* (dedicated to Sanford) was inspired by hearing a group of Welsh singers at a distance in Cardiganshire in 1901 [2] and perhaps again later nearer the Wye.[3] Though the falling third occurs in many Welsh hymn tunes, the most likely theme here, as Mr Alan Webb, curator of the Birthplace, has suggested, is 'Land of my Fathers',

[1] *Op. cit.*, p. 46.
[2] Percy Young, *Elgar O.M.*, p. 293.
[3] Reed (*op. cit.*, p. 85) is wrong when he says Malvern.

the Welsh National Anthem (second half). The middle section of
the work is one of the things the composer enjoyed: 'A devil of a
fugue . . . with all sorts of japes and counterpoint.' 'Jape' was a
characteristically Elgarian word. In the main, however, the work
is sadly grand, with a tremendous feeling for sound, without
theorizing.

When Elgar was given the freedom of the city of Worcester on
12th September 1905 he walked in procession wearing the Yale
University gown and hood, while his father, now unable to leave
his room (he died early the next year), watched from an upstairs
window. Elgar turned and saluted him as he passed.

During the latter part of the year and early in 1906 Elgar was
busy on a second oratorio to follow *The Apostles*, using some of the
same material: *The Kingdom*. He intended that there should be
three works but was too discouraged to complete the third part of
the trilogy. When he had overcome initial inertia he worked
extremely hard: his concentration and utter detachment from the
world while on the soprano passage, 'The sun goeth down', are
well described by Dorabella.[1] This was also the time when he
enjoyed his chemistry experiments, which were a relaxation from
composition. *The Kingdom* was produced at the Birmingham
Festival in October, conducted by the composer in New York in
March 1907 and then in other parts of the United States.

In June 1907 Lord Northampton came to stay at Plas Gwyn
and he sometimes played the pedal parts of Bach's organ music at
the piano while Elgar played the rest.[2] He was another encouraging
friend for whom Elgar 'felt better'. In a letter of 15th August 1904
the former had written: 'You have in you a special power of
bringing upon others the strongest influence for good. . . . You
have moved men's souls to the highest truths of Christianity',[3] but
even Northampton could not get Elgar to write the third oratorio,
of which there were sketches waiting to be used. Others tried, and

[1] Powell, *op. cit.*, pp. 69–72.

[2] Young, *op. cit.*, p. 136.

[3] Quoted by Kennedy, *op. cit.*, p. 165 (see also pp. 168 and 169).

he made half-hearted attempts right up to his seventieth birthday, but with no result.

Apart from small pieces and a fourth *Pomp and Circumstance* march, Elgar next became absorbed in some of his early sketches dating back to 1867 and wrote two suites based on them called *The Wand of Youth*, though his mind had long been working on a symphonic project, with the idea of characterizing Gordon in it. Ultimately he used no character in the Symphony for Full Orchestra, Op. 55,[1] which was first performed under Richter in Manchester in December 1908. Only four days later it was given in London. Richter, to whom it was dedicated, addressed the orchestra: 'Gentlemen, let us now rehearse the greatest symphony of modern times, written by the greatest modern composer,' and he added, '*and not only in this country.*'[2] (One sign of Elgar's continuity of thought has been pointed out by Reed: the motto theme with which this Symphony opens is foreshadowed in the first violins at the very end of the *Enigma Variations*, fig. 82,[3] though he was sketching it, as if new, in Italy in December 1907.[4]) The work was received with enormous enthusiasm and there were nearly a hundred performances of it in Britain during its first year. During the next two years it went all over Europe. Jaeger, ill and now with less than a year to live, when he had looked at the score wrote that it had the greatest slow movement since Beethoven. It was, as Kennedy has noted, not only Elgar's but England's first symphony.

The beginning of 1909 was somewhat fallow, but another visit to Italy produced the part-songs 'Angelus (Tuscany)', Op. 56, and 'Go, Song of Mine', Op. 57. In May 1909 Elgar wrote some of his tiniest pieces: two single and two double chants. At least one of the former (in the *New Cathedral Psalter*) has an Elgarian touch—not easy in such an apparently simple medium. An *Elegy*, Op. 58, for string orchestra followed the news of the death of his great

---

[1] See letter to Walford Davies, 13th November 1908.

[2] Reed, *op. cit.*, p. 97.

[3] *Ibid.*, pp. 156, 157.

[4] McVeagh, *op. cit.*, p. 49.

champion, Jaeger, though it was not actually in his memory. Richter's performance of 'Nimrod' was a greater tribute—the first of many funeral occasions on which this solemn variation has been played. Most of Elgar's works were dedicated to his friends but usually the composition had started some time before the dedication, or—if one allows the absurd idea of the variation 'G.R.S.' representing not the organist Sinclair but his bulldog Dan— rededication.

Another puzzle arose over the Violin Concerto, Op. 61 (on which he had started work in February 1910), although it was clearly dedicated to Fritz Kreisler, who gave the first performance in November 1910. W. H. Reed had been with the composer, giving technical advice as violinist both in London and in 'The Hut' near Maidenhead belonging to another friend, Frank Schuster. On the score is the inscription in Spanish: 'Aquí está encerrada el alma de . . . . .' (Here is enshrined the soul of . . . . .). The five dots were thought to be the Christian name of an American friend, Julia Worthington.[1] Dunhill [2] does not even bother to copy out more than three dots, while Reed actually uses eight.[3] It was not 'Fritz' or 'Frank' because, according to Ernest Newman,[4] Elgar had assured Basil Maine that it was feminine. According to Percy Young [5] it could have been Adela Schuster or many others. According to Kennedy [6] it is much more likely to have been Alice StuartWortley, daughter of Millais and second wife of Lord Stuart of Wortley, who was closely associated with Elgar and his music at this time. In fact between 1909 and 1931 he wrote her more than four hundred letters; all the sketches of the concerto went to her; the second subject is quoted on the occasion of the anniversary of starting work; and it, and others, are called 'windflower themes', since he always referred to her by this drooping woodanemone's

[1] Powell, *op. cit.*, p. 86; McVeagh, *op. cit.*, pp. 53 and 54.
[2] Thomas Dunhill, *Sir Edward Elgar* (1938), p. 138.
[3] W. H. Reed, *Elgar as I knew him* (1936), p. 154.
[4] In the *Sunday Times*, 21st May 1939.
[5] *Op. cit.*, p. 335.
[6] *Op. cit.*, p. 129.

name. When Reed went to Schuster's, he met many Elgar wor-
shippers and the first he named was Mrs Stuart-Wortley.[1] A
granddaughter of Millais, Mrs Perrine Moncrieff, recalls that once
when she visited her aunt Alice a stiff servant stopped her with:
'Yes, her Ladyship is in. But you can't go up, Miss: Sir Edward
Elgar is with her.'

The maturing man and the changing relationship is shown if
one compares a very early, typically 'silly' letter of 10th June 1903
with one of 23rd February 1920. In the former, he 'flirts' as he did
with most of the ladies of the *Variations*, and says how sorry he was
that 'goodnight' was not said and wanting forgiveness for '(A)
not saying "goodnight" prettily (B) for sending such a long letter
(C) for not knowing your name; it must be a "nice" one . . .'.
Brought up sharply by the harsh realities of the world six weeks
before his beloved wife's death, he wrote the following very
different letter seventeen years later:

My dear W. [Windflower]

It seems weary ages since I saw or heard of you: things are very dull
and my poor dear Alice does not really improve in strength, so after all
I did not go to Stoke; it seemed too lonely for her. Carice will be back
indoors a fortnight and we shall see what can be done.

I have just been down to the club a few times and tried a lonely
theatre on occasion but everything seemed dreadfully commonplace and
awful! I go to the Gramophone tomorrow and have several silly
meetings, etc.—it is a brainless soulless existence and I wonder very
often what it is all about and why it is so—but so it is. Do ring up
sometime—I want to go to *Pygmalion* one day—wd that do for you?

Felix was here yesterday eveg and delighted at the prospect of going
to you.

Have you played the Sonata with Reed yet or again?

Love yours

E.

Many writers have apologized for Elgar's vocal compositions,
and he was clearly a man who thought first of instruments,

[1] *Op. cit.*, p. 27.

although at this time he did work with Ivor Atkins, organist of Worcester, on a new and excellent edition of Bach's *St Matthew Passion*. Jaeger objected to several things in *The Apostles* connected with word-setting, none of which was altered by the obstinate composer. Typical was the repeated 'cometh' on p. 135 of the vocal score, in a typically orchestral thought during Judas's betrayal scene. A purely orchestral work would show Elgar at his best; a work, moreover, with solo violin was to show him at the height of his powers. Some composers write with caution and even tameness for the instrument that they themselves have played. Not so Elgar. The solo part is fiendishly difficult. But it is violinist's music and full of intense emotion—a portrait rather than a land-scape.

George V succeeded Edward VII in 1910; 1911 was Corona-tion Year. Alice was delighted to watch her husband enter the temple of fame and at the same time to see him climbing even higher up the social ladder. Five days before the coronation Elgar received the Order of Merit and his Symphony No. 2, Op. 63, was produced. Much time had been spent on its composition in different places: most years in this period of his life he visited Italy and the U.S.A. It was dedicated to the memory of Edward VII and the score is prefaced with some lines from Shelley: 'Rarely, rarely, comest thou, Spirit of Delight!' Although the symphony contains some of Elgar's finest music—particularly the intimate slow movement—it did not appeal to the public as the Symphony No. 1 and the Violin Concerto had done. This was noticed with disappointment by the composer.

Early in 1912 the Elgars moved to a Hampstead house (which they called Severn House) because they felt the need to be in London to cope with the large number of engagements and to be near many influential people. Also Edward liked the theatre and his clubs in London. Using up some old material and breaking off from time to time to play billiards or use his microscope, he completed the music for the masque *The Crown of India,* which was performed at the London Coliseum in March. The occasion was George V's visit to India. The next work, also using old material, was *The Music Makers*; the difference was, however, that this time the listener could recognize an almost embarrassing number of well known themes from the composer's greatest works. Charles Proctor, who has given sympathetic performances of this setting of O'Shaughnessy's ode, suggests that one should think of these self-quotations as one thinks of a small boy who invites you up to his bedroom to show you his 'treasures': string, penknife and so on. Some ear trouble which had interfered with Elgar's work was treated and cleared up by the end of May and *The Music Makers* was first performed in Birmingham on October 1st.

While in Italy early in 1913 Elgar started seriously accumulating sketches for a musical study of Shakespeare's Falstaff: the knight, gentleman and soldier of Henry IV, not the buffoon of *The Merry Wives of Windsor*, as already treated by Nicolai and Verdi. His views are given in an analytical essay in the *Musical Times*, 1913. Elgar was extremely well-informed on Shakespeare: see, for example, his letter on 'Scott and Shakespeare' to *The Times Literary Supplement* of 21st July 1921. He conducted the first performance in October at the Leeds Festival and thought it to be his best orchestral work. This was his last major contribution to composition before the outbreak of World War I when, at the age of fifty-seven, he was a great and respected figure throughout the musical world. He was toying not only with the idea of a third oratorio but also with the possibility of writing an opera and—less enthusiastically—with a piano concerto, but to no effect. The Elgars were holidaying in Ross-shire when war was declared. When they returned 'Land of Hope and Glory' had become once more the composer's most popular piece.

CHAPTER IV

THE THIRD PERIOD: THE CHAMBER

IN THE earlier part of 1914 Elgar wrote some small orchestral pieces—*Carissima* (the first of his works to be recorded), *Rosemary* and (more seriously) *Sospiri*—and a setting of Psalm xxix, 'Give unto the Lord', performed at St Paul's in April. Soon, however, he had to exchange his conductor's baton for that of a special constable. He was too old to be a soldier but he was willing to serve his country. Most biographers have quoted either with no comment or with embarrassment a letter he wrote to Frank Schuster on 25th August 1914. Since, however, I share Elgar's view that it is more sinful to torture animals than humans, I have some sympathy with the feelings expressed in the following extract from that letter: 'The only thing that wrings my heart and soul is the thought of the horses—oh! my beloved animals—the men—and women can go to hell—but my horses; I walk round and round this room cursing God for allowing dumb beasts to be tortured— let Him kill his human beings but—how CAN HE? Oh, my horses.' With very few exceptions this was to be the last time that horses were actually to be used in cavalry action (as opposed to ordinary pack duties), though Elgar was not to know this.

In Rome in December 1907 his horror of pain and suffering had showed itself in a strangely tortured part-song called 'Owls', for which he wrote the words himself. Frightened of being laughed at, he made not only the words and the music obscure but also the dedication, which was to 'my friend Pietro d'Alba' (his daughter's white Peter Rabbit): 'A wild thing hurt but mourns in the night. ... What is it? Nothing,' he says. The following April, in a letter to Jaeger, he laughed it off as only a fantasy, but obviously it was not.

During the war Elgar wrote a number of patriotic pieces, songs, choral and orchestral works and several settings of recitations by the Belgian poet, Émile Cammaerts. After Belgium, he turned his attention to Poland, again to help refugees, together with his friend Paderewski, the great pianist who later became Prime Minister of Poland. Themes from Paderewski and Chopin are quoted in *Polonia*, Op. 76, first performed at the Queen's Hall, London, in July 1915. In 1915 Elgar resigned from the Special Constabulary and joined the Hampstead Volunteer Reserve: now he had a rifle instead of a baton. Alice and Carice were also doing war work, but they had time for entertaining and Edward still enjoyed art, drama and old books.

The settings of Binyon started in 1915 with 'To Women' and 'For the Fallen'. With the addition of the weaker 'The Fourth of August', they were put together under the title of *The Spirit of England* and performed collectively in London in November 1917. There had been a misunderstanding with Cyril Rootham, who also set and published 'For the Fallen', and it may well be that the lack of enthusiasm for Elgar's music in Cambridge—already Stanford had cooled—increased at this time. 'The academics who held Elgar down until he had reached his forties had fortunately no stronger weapon than a common dislike which found vent in systematic disparagement,' said Sir Richard Terry.[1] In 1930 Edward Dent, Professor of Music at Cambridge, contributed a distinctly cool appraisal of Elgar to Adler's *Handbuch der Musik-geschichte*.[2]

A complete contrast in these grim times was the writing of incidental music to a fanciful play, *The Starlight Express* by Violet Pearn, based on a book by Algernon Blackwood and first per-formed in December 1915. Another work of this kind was a ballet, *The Sanguine Fan*, first performed in March 1917, after which Elgar returned to the war with *The Fringes of the Fleet* in June. This also involved a good deal of conducting, both in London and in the provinces.

[1] See Cecil Gray, *Peter Warlock* (1934), p. 268.

[2] See Kennedy, *op. cit.*, p. 261, and Basil Maine, *Elgar: his Life and Work* (1933), vol. i, pp. 277 foll.

Among those who died in 1917 were Elgar's uncle, Henry, and his old friend of Hereford Cathedral, George Sinclair. Lady Elgar noted that her husband thought much about the latter, as he contemplated his last letter. Now came a withdrawal from the hurly-burly of the metropolis to Sussex to write chamber music. There was even a withdrawal from his former self.[1] Brinkwells is a thatched cottage off a secluded winding lane which runs from Fittleworth to Wisborough Green. From a studio in the garden there was a beautiful view. Fifty years later the roof was leaking badly and there was a threat of demolition but, thanks to the generosity of a lady who wishes to remain anonymous, the roof was re-thatched in the autumn of 1967 and so the cottage has been saved for a further spell in a setting still remarkably unchanged and unspoilt. Lady Elgar and Carice did not always enjoy the remoteness and the lack of amenities, but for Edward the stimulus came to write new and more intimate music.

Early in 1918 Elgar had a tonsil operation and while in the nursing home started sketches for a string quartet; then at Severn House he started planning a violin and piano sonata. Ultimately, at Brinkwells, he was working on three chamber works: Sonata in E minor, Op. 82, for violin and piano, String Quartet in E minor, Op. 83, and Piano Quintet in A minor, Op. 84. All three works were performed in London the following year. The woods at Flexham Park, with a legend of impious Spanish monks who were turned into withered trees, exercised a strange power over him as he wrote (but see page 77).

There was alternatively serenity and psychic disturbance, sometimes producing what Reed aptly describes as 'languid melancholy'[2] in the second subject of the Piano Quintet, where the austere first subject, converted, seems to take on an almost Spanish flavour—not, I think, a 'semi-oriental mood' as Reed suggests, unless one accepts the Moorish influence in Spain. Elgar also enjoyed his pipe and other compensations. 'You will be amused to learn,' he writes, 'that I get Beer here in "plural quantities" as O.

[1] Young, *op. cit.*, p. 191.
[2] *Op. cit.*, p. 125.

Henry says. It seems strange after the difficulties in London. . . . It is lovely to hear the birds—nightingales abound and their song is really the most lovely thing in nature. . . .'[1] While still completing the chamber works he started composing the Cello Concerto, and carried on with its composition at Severn House in October.

Reed first played the Sonata with, as pianist, Landon Ronald, who at the time was one of the finest conductors of Elgar's orchestral music.[2] Then he played second violin to Albert Sammons (the British String Quartet) when all three chamber works were splendidly performed on 21st May 1919 at the Wigmore Hall. The cellist was Felix Salmond, who not only later tried over the new concerto with the composer but was the soloist for the first performance with the London Symphony Orchestra at the Queen's Hall in October. A nineteenyearold cellist, John Barbirolli, was in the orchestra. The public did not show great excitement about this strange melancholy work, with its frequent strainings towards optimism but equally numerous moments of resignation—in the long drawnout slow passage just before the end of the finale, in particular. The work was also underrehearsed.[3]

Elgar's close association, if not infatuation, with Alice StuartWortley, a lady five years younger than himself, the discreet supperparties, the visits to the opera, the fishing expeditions, were borne with a politician's indifference by Lord Stuart of Wortley. They were tolerated also by Lady Elgar, but at this time can hardly have increased her will to live. Earlier biographers seem to have been totally unaware of, or singularly discreet about, this strange episode. One can only suppose that Lady Stuart of Wortley inspired the Violin Concerto as Mathilde Wesendonck did *Tristan*; it is possible for a composer to be inspired by a woman who is not his wife, without the suspicion of a dishonourable liaison. Jelly D'Aranyi, not only a fine violinist but also an attractive young lady

[1] Letter to Lady Stuart of Wortley, 7th May 1918.

[2] Dorabella (Mrs R. Powell) wrote to E. A. Butcher on 26th January 1955: 'Landon Ronald was certainly a very fine conductor and interpreter of Elgar and there is not his equal now in England.'

[3] Kennedy, *op. cit.*, p. 235.

of twenty-six in 1919, did not much enjoy Elgar's company or attention [1] and consequently, it seems, she did not like his concerto.

Back in Severn House, which they were finding expensive to run, Elgar became occupied again with his microscope and with visits to the zoo. There were more honours, more conducting, being filmed for the first time, the appreciation of Bernard Shaw and the thrill of Symphony No. 2 under a new conductor, Adrian Boult, who was to be identified with Elgar's music as no one else. 'How beautiful to have this and the Symphony success—so thankful,' wrote Alice, for the last time, in her diary. There was no new composition. Instead there was foreboding. After a short illness, Alice died on 7th April 1920, at the age of 71. Sammons, Reed, Jeremy and, for Salmond, Patterson Parker [2] played the slow movement of the String Quartet at the funeral, which took place at St Wulstan's Roman Catholic Church, Little Malvern, near the pre-Cambrian volcanic rocks of the Herefordshire Beacon and not far from Craeg Lea. It seems that Reed was so upset that he did not know who was playing with him. He said in his first book [3]: 'I hurriedly arranged this: and Sammons, Tertis, Salmond and I went to Malvern and played.' In fact Tertis sent his talented pupil, Raymond Jeremy, which was noted by Reed in his second book,[4] and Parker was substituted for Felix Salmond.

Added to Elgar's personal sense of loss was the bitterness in knowing that his daughter Carice [5] would inherit nothing from the 'awful aunts': 'a wretched lot of old incompetents simply because I was—well—I.' [6] Alice, it may be remembered, had married the son of a mere tuner, a tradesman who had called at the back door of her upper-class family, some of whom had actually disinherited her on her marriage. What an ironic situation that

[1] Joseph Macleod, *The Sisters D'Aranyi* (1969), pp. 116–19.

[2] McVeagh, *op. cit.*, p. 69.

[3] *Elgar as I knew him* (1936), p. 67.

[4] *Elgar* (1939), p. 131.

[5] She was married to Samuel Blake on 16th January 1922.

[6] Letter to Frank Schuster, 17th April 1920.

when she died Elgar was a friend of royalty and at the top of the social hierarchy!

After the war the revived Three Choirs Festival at Worcester in 1920 included the Elgar-Atkins edition of the *St Matthew Passion*. There were few other occasions on which the conditions of the original performance, at Leipzig with two organs, had been reproduced, observes Watkins Shaw.[1] A Wagnerian touch was added by playing a chorale before each part by brass from the top of the Cathedral tower, as in Elgar's arrangement of 1911. Elgar now buried himself in his hobbies as much as he could but creatively his life was empty. 'I feel like these woods [Brinkwells] —all aglow,' he wrote in July 1921, 'a spark wd. start a flame— but no human spark comes.'[2] But a more cheerful letter of the same date to Lady Stuart of Wortley quoted a German in his '*best English*': '"the celestial unearthly Quintet that to hear I had the occasion only *one meal*"—meaning, of course, *ein mal*'.

He enjoyed recording for H.M.V. at Hayes and in April 1921, a year after his bereavement, he orchestrated Bach's organ Fugue in C minor, the fulfilment of a promise made to Richard Strauss in 1902. Later he added the Fantasia, to demonstrate how the modern orchestra could be used to show off these works. To Eugene Goossens, who conducted the first performance of the Fugue at the Queen's Hall in October 1921, he confessed that now only the works of J. S. Bach inspired him to think musically.[3] He left Severn House and lived in a London flat for two years, going the rounds of his clubs, which now included Brooks's. He went on a cruise to South America and a thousand miles up the Amazon in November 1923, after having already leased a new house back in his own county of Worcestershire.

Elgar conducted his *Empire March*, not as planned at the opening ceremony of the British Empire Exhibition at Wembley in April 1924, but later in the year at the Pageant. In June he had a strenuous tour of central and north Wales. At the fifth Aberystwyth

[1] *Op. cit.*, p. 94.
[2] Letter to Sir Sidney Colvin, 27th July 1921.
[3] Eugene Goossens, *Overture and Beginners* (1951).

Festival the Cello Concerto was played by Joachim-trained Arthur Williams, who was particularly good in the slow movement (he had played it before in 1923); two days later Elgar was conducting *The Apostles* at Harlech. He had to stop a little man who started to make a speech and it needed all the tact and charm of Walford Davies to soothe him.[1] He noted with regret the deaths of Fauré and Puccini this year. On the death of Sir Walter Parratt the position of Master of the King's Musick fell vacant and Elgar was appointed in May 1924 to this important but not exacting post. The next year he received the gold medal of the Royal Philharmonic Society.

His love of animals, especially dogs, was so strong in this retirement period that it was said that he used to ring up his Worcestershire house from Brooks's just in order to hear his dogs barking.[2] He was happy if he could see the wild birds feeding within thirty yards of his window, as he wrote from Scotland to Lady Stuart of Wortley in 1914, and resented it if 'progress' made it no longer possible for birds to nest in the eaves of his house. 'I think I could turn and live with animals,' wrote Whitman in a poem of which Elgar was particularly fond. He was in most respects a Conservative. Politically he opposed the beginning of Socialism, while he loved and romanticized the past both in his behaviour and, as can be seen, in his works. He seemed to know every inch of his native county and never tired of re-exploring it.[3] With silvery hair and moustache he roamed the countryside looking, but not feeling, like a local squire. He still conducted from time to time, with an 'uneasy wilful beat',[4] yet 'he could make you feel exactly what he wanted if you were in sympathy with him'[5] and he had an expressive left hand. He did not like other people's interpretations,[6]

---

[1] Ian Parrott, *The Spiritual Pilgrims* (Llandybie, 1969), p. 62.

[2] Charles Graves, *Leather Armchairs* (1963).

[3] W. H. Reed, *Elgar as I knew him* (1936).

[4] 'C' in the *Musical Times*, June 1926.

[5] John Barbirolli, 'A Personal Note' in the L.P. recording of *Gerontius*, E.M.I., 1965.

[6] See his letter of 1st June 1903 to Jaeger.

he seemed 'frigid' when compared with Henry Wood,[1] and yet he astonished with the 'magic powers of his personality . . . all performers are controlled by a great mind from the moment he raises his baton'.[2] His only compositions at this time were either slight, 'occasional' or arrangements, although he thought of writing an opera. Between 1927 and 1929 he moved twice to other houses not far away before settling down in the last one, Marl Bank, on the edge of the city of Worcester.

[1] *Sheffield Telegraph*, 3rd October 1902.
[2] *Birmingham Post*, 10th September 1931.

CHAPTER V

THE LAST YEARS: RETIREMENT

IN THE year 1928 Elgar was created K.C.V.O., and received the Cobbett Medal for Chamber Music. Also his oboe-playing brother, Frank, died. When Elgar left the Theatre Royal, Birmingham, after conducting the first performance of the *Beau Brummel* incidental music on 5th November 1928, a reporter asked him, 'Have you any faith in Choral Singing in this country in the future?', to which he replied, 'I have no faith in anything,' and slammed the taxi door.

A new pleasure for him was the gramophone, while an old one was going to the races. He saw an increasing amount of Bernard Shaw at about this time and it was through him that the B.B.C. was persuaded to commission a third symphony for £1,000. For many years Shaw had expressed himself forcibly as an anti-vivisectionist and his protest was particularly strong at this time; [1] thus he gained a bond of sympathy with Elgar, animal-lover as well as play-goer. He also recommended osteopathy for Elgar's lumbago.

The lonely composer really loved his dogs. Mr Wulstan Atkins, son of the organist of Worcester Cathedral, remembers the dogs at mealtimes sitting on chairs on either side of the composer. In human company the composer was sometimes moody and impolite. The first appearance of the New York Philharmonic Orchestra in London under Toscanini was a memorable occasion for all who can remember it. After a thrilling performance of the *Enigma Variations* on 2nd June 1930 Harriet Cohen went up to Elgar at the Savoy Grill and burst out with 'Wasn't it mar-

[1] See 'The Shavian Approach to Medical Reform', *Medical News*, 13th November 1964.

vellous?' 'What was marvellous?' he asked, stonily. 'The concert,' she faltered. 'What concert?' he said, and sat down without a further word.[1]

In 1930 there were signs of a new lease of life, however, when in April the *Severn Suite*, Op. 87, was completed for the annual brass-band contest held at the Crystal Palace. This work, dedicated to Shaw, was later arranged by the composer for orchestra. Shaw advised him to drop the polite Italian indications and suggested bandsman's language: 'Remember that a minuet is a dance and not a bloody hymn; or Steady up for artillery attack; or Now—like hell.' [2] The *Severn Suite* contains passages marked to be played muted for euphoniums, but at the time no euphonium mutes existed: [3] they had to be made specially for the Crystal Palace contest. The results were not very satisfactory and the experiment has not been repeated. With the military band the composer was completely at ease. Many were the times when he would drive to Kneller Hall with the Duke of Connaught, whose estate at Richmond was near by. He enjoyed in particular listening to the students playing the wind version of *Cockaigne*. The next work, finished the following year, was dedicated to the Princesses Elizabeth (later Queen) and Margaret and their mother, then the Duchess of York. The *Nursery Suite*, first performed in June 1931, also made use of old sketches; it was later made into a ballet by Ninette de Valois.

Another thing gave the ageing composer a new zest for life: his friendship with the fifteen-year-old violinist, Yehudi Menuhin, who gave a historic performance of the Violin Concerto, with Elgar conducting, in November 1932. Elgar's seventy-fifth birthday (June) was celebrated by the B.B.C. with three concerts in December and he started work on the third symphony and on an opera: Sir Barry Jackson [4] helped to compile a libretto from a book

[1] Harriet Cohen, *A Bundle of Time* (1969), p. 166.

[2] Letter of 28th September 1930.

[3] Denis Wright, *The Complete Bandmaster* (1963), p. 148.

[4] See his article in *Music and Letters*, January 1943.

of Elgar's choice, Ben Jonson's *The Devil is an Ass*, and the work was to be called *The Spanish Lady*. In May 1933, Menuhin performed the Violin Concerto again in Paris; Elgar travelled for the first time by plane and before the concert visited the paralysed Delius at Grez. Both composers had only one more year to live. 'To me,' wrote Elgar,[1] 'he seemed like the poet who, seeing the sun again after his pilgrimage, had found complete harmony between will and desire.' The recording made at this time of Menuhin's performance of the concerto remained in the catalogues until January 1955, and it was to appear later on an L.P. disc. The boy's understanding was remarkable not only because of his age but also because of his completely different background.[2] He was able to impress even the most insular of nations, the French, although he was partly helped by the selfless preparation of the resident conductor in Paris, Georges Enesco.[3]

In October 1933 Elgar went to a nursing home in Worcester and was found to be suffering from a malignant tumour which pressed on the sciatic nerve; from now on he was to have periods of intense pain, in between which he thought about his third symphony. However this, like the opera, was to be merely sketches. Although he recovered somewhat and returned to Marl Bank after Christmas, he grew steadily weaker. Just as he enjoyed the gramophone—his bedroom was connected by microphone with a London recording studio—so he also enjoyed the radio. In particular, unlike most people, he liked to turn the controls down for the softest possible sounds. He had written a little essay (found among his papers) called 'H.M.V.' in which he extolled the 'marvel' of the gramophone, which 'makes study so much easier and makes the waste of so much time and energy [his early journeys to London] unnecessary'. On 23rd February 1934 he died.

Since some doubt has been expressed on Elgar's faith at the end

[1] In the *Daily Telegraph*, 1st July 1933.
[2] Maine, *op. cit.*, i, p. 264.
[3] H. A. Chambers (ed.), *Edward Elgar, Centenary Sketches* (1957), p. 30.

of his life, a letter from his daughter to the *Musical Times* of January 1969 needs quoting: 'Father Gibb S.J. from St George's, Worcester, was asked to attend, and to him my father re-affirmed his faith in the Roman Catholic Church.' Peter J. Pirie, in a letter in the same issue, confirms this, adding the significant comment that Elgar 'would utter extravagant things under provocation or pain'. After the disastrous first performance of *Gerontius*, for example, he wrote that his heart was now 'shut against every religious feeling and every soft, gentle impulse *for ever*'.[1] But if he had moved away from 'orthodoxy' it was, thought Percy Young,[2] not because he had too little faith but because he had too much. Ernest Newman wrote in the *Sunday Times* of 13th November 1955 that he had visited Elgar a few days before his death: 'Then, after a brief silence, he made a single short remark about himself which I have never disclosed to anyone and have no intention of ever disclosing, for it would lend itself too easily to the crudest of misinterpretations at the hands of thick-fingered psychologists.' As a last effort in 1970 I asked Newman's widow if she had been told but, alas, Newman had been as enigmatic as Elgar, so the reader must continue to speculate. The comment may have concerned Elgar's relationship with his wife, I venture to think, but it may equally well have been about his music or his religious doubts.

He was buried as he had wished, beside his wife at St Wulstan's Church, Little Malvern, and not near the junction of the rivers Teme and Severn which had also been considered. A memorial service was held in Worcester Cathedral. The same year his birth-place was bought by Worcester Corporation, the first step in the establishment of a museum, and on the first day of the Three Choirs Festival of 1935 a cathedral window, designed by A. K. Nicholson, was dedicated to Elgar's memory. Written tributes to him were not always consistent. Constant Lambert declared that Elgar was 'the first English composer since the eighteenth century who was the technical equal of his foreign contemporaries', whilst

[1] Letter of 9th October 1900 to Jaeger.
[2] *Op. cit.*, p. 255.

Arnold Bax commented [1] that 'He may be described as the last of the classics' and Kreisler said: [2] 'Elgar was great—the last, perhaps, of the great romantic composers.' Most of his belongings, heirlooms, honours and paraphernalia are still to be seen at the cottage birth-place, which was reopened in May 1967 by Yehudi Menuhin.

[1] *Daily Telegraph*, 26th February 1934.
[2] *Daily Telegraph*, 1st March 1934.

CHAPTER VI

CANTATAS AND OTHER CHORAL WORKS

LUDWIG UHLAND (1787–1862), though not one of Germany's greatest poets, had his verses set by such composers as Mendelssohn, Schumann and Brahms. The 'horrific' romanticism of his *Der Schwarze Ritter* appealed to the young Elgar who, like many another enthusiastic young composer, did not wait to decide what impact any musical setting would have but simply used the lines to release his creative energy. Even at this early stage (1890–2) his feeling for instruments was ahead both of his sense of the appropriate and of his personal individuality. Not surprisingly he describes *The Black Knight* (in Longfellow's 'broken-backed, spavined' [1] translation) as a 'Symphony for Chorus and Orchestra' and not a 'Choral Ballad'. Though Reed admired much of the dramatic chromatic writing [2] it is nearly all derivative, and the word-setting is sometimes awkward. Schumann, Mendelssohn, Chopin and others have their echoes. Some of the most elegant music is what has later been called 'light'—e.g. in sc. 3—and this is sturdily un-Wagnerian. Does the second dance here, with its curious Spanish rhythm, anticipate the odd motive later not very well adapted to Gerontius on his death-bed (see No. 4)? A wholly delightful pastiche of 1895 is the set of 'choral songs' *From the Bavarian Highlands*, in which the composer and his wife collaborated in music and words to imitate Bavarian *Volkslieder* and *Schnadahüpfler*, which they did with gusto and brilliance.

Not only in its use of an orchestral introduction but in other ways too *The Light of Life* (*Lux Christi*, early 1896) anticipates *Gerontius*. Although Elgar seems still to treat the chorus as an appendage, he is developing a most sensitive Italianate attitude

[1] Ernest Newman, *Elgar* (1905), p. 10.
[2] *Op. cit.*, p. 38.

towards the solo voice. He is not yet using very small units but he displays his material in the opening 'Meditation'—quite short ideas of eight to a dozen bars each—immediately and he is rich in invention; there is little padding or marking time. An Elgarian habit is soon noticed: the two inner parts move in octaves. The story of Jesus healing the blind man was adapted by the Rev. E. Capel/Cure and Elgar seems to identify himself to some extent with the blind man's suffering in a way that he was to again with the death throes of Gerontius. If he writes in eight parts and if he manages a four/square fugue (in No. 9)—to the rather appropriate words, 'The wisdom of their wise men shall perish'—without adding to his stature today, it must be remembered that at that period this was expected of any respectable oratorio writer. Elgar was to be dogged for many years by the taunts that he was not as good at this sort of thing as Parry, Stanford and others. After a while he went his own way as a composer, but he never forgot the taunts.

The unaccompanied part/song 'As torrents in summer', already in print, was pasted into the manuscript full score of *Scenes from the Saga of King Olaf*, after which the practical com/poser wrote the significant words: 'Pause for lost pitch'. Before this somewhat Sullivanesque epilogue there is some powerful music despite the lame, tame verses of Longfellow, which are helped out by some of H. A. Acworth's. The vigour of the tales of the Norse/men is a challenge to the composer as Thor is a challenge to Olaf and there is much that is pictorial in the music, much of it hearty in a pagan way, though at 'Olaf bore the cross to the folk at Nidaros' (Acworth), there is a chorale/like motive, later used to represent the Christian influence. More striking harmonically is the motive associated with Odin the Goth, forebear of Ironbeard, who is slain by Olaf; yet Christianity, with its weaker music, ultimately prevails. The work is divided into some well/constructed separate choral numbers and the composer's invention runs high, especially attractive being the ballad 'A little bird in the air' (Thyri, No. 13), which is like a scherzo; and much of the writing generally is pro/phetic of the greater Elgar to come. It was intended, said the com/

34

poser, that the performers should be looked upon as a gathering of *skalds* (bards)—all in turn taking part in the narration of the saga and occasionally, at the more dramatic points, personifying for the moment some important character. This, not really operatic thinking, became Elgar's general method. (The relics of the historic Olaf, King of Norway, killed 1030, are enshrined in the cathedral at Trondhjem—in 1930 the ancient name of Nidaros was re-introduced.)

The cantata *Caractacus*, written for the Leeds Festival of 1898, although exhibiting some fine moments, does not show as much development of Elgar's individuality as one would expect. The last stand of the British chieftain offers as much dramatic stuff as before, but Caractacus is still a Wagnerian hero and when his daughter, Eigen, enters (fig. 33) the music, losing its Siegfried-like, flat-keys panache, softens to G major as if it were Gutrune who steps upon the stage (see *Götterdämmerung*, Act I, sc. 2, her second appearance). Much of the chorus work in the second scene is devised on lines which Sullivan used more than once in his operas: the men sing their theme, then the women, then both together. Eigen's betrothed lover, Orbin, moreover, has a feeble *leitmotiv* reminiscent of 'I have a song to sing-O',[1] which is not very inspiring. The work is peppered with stage directions such as 'He casts down his harp and rushes off', but these are normally purely imaginary. Once, however, the work was actually staged as an opera, serving, as Percy Young [2] has noted, to show that it lacks 'compulsive dramatic movement'. It is surprising how unoriginal much of *Caractacus* is. Scene 5, the lament at the chief-tain's capture, is very Brahmsian, but fortunately scene 6 recovers, although Caractacus is now paraded ignominiously before the Emperor Claudius in Rome, who pardons him. Final choral praise not for the Roman Empire but for the British was described by Maine as 'incongruous' [3] and by Newman as 'a serious blot on the dramatic scheme' and 'the cantata is thus made to end in a

[1] *The Yeomen of the Guard*, 1888.
[2] *Op. cit.*, p. 299.
[3] *Op. cit.*, ii, p. 32.

sputter of bathos and rant'. However, patriotic sentiment at this time was something very real. Elgar had already shared in it in the short 'ballad' of 1897, *The Banner of St George*, and he was to express it again in the *Coronation Ode* of 1902.

Some of the broader, lyrical middle sections of his vigorous choral set pieces impressed themselves on the styles of such men as Bax and Ireland, for example the part at No. 4, *cantabile e larga-mente*, in the splendid Triumphal Procession which opens sc. 6 of *Caractacus*. Elgar made the Romans see into the future in a very odd way by anticipating the British Empire, but Ireland wrote similar *cantabile* music in *These Things Shall Be* (1936), and his view of international brotherhood was anything but imperialistic.

After the three great oratorios (see Chapter IX), Elgar wrote very little substantial choral music. The ode *The Music Makers*, a setting of O'Shaughnessy, dates from 1912, although sketches go back more than four years, while the three Binyon settings called *The Spirit of England* date from war-time 1916. Although these works with their assured technique are effective in performance, they do not materially add very much to the composer's reputation; indeed the former serves to remind the listener of his greater works by extensive use of self-quotation. These, eight in number, are listed by Kennedy.[1]

[1] *Op. cit.*, p. 298.

CHAPTER VII

THE 'ENIGMA VARIATIONS': THE MUSIC
AND THE PROBLEM

FROM the earliest days Elgar showed an inclination towards the tonality of G major-minor. His earliest surviving work is probably an unfinished Fugue in G minor of about 1870. The alternation of a minor key with its tonic major was not a particulare featur of the practice of the classical masters before Schubert, but it does happen to be the scheme of the Menuetto and Trio of Mozart's Symphony No. 40 in G minor. In 1878 Elgar started to write a paraphrase of this work. That he apparently broke off before reaching the Minuet need not concern us; the pattern was established [1] and he used the key of G, fluctuating between minor and major in such large works as *King Olaf, Lux Christi* and the Organ Sonata, employing or suggesting also a *tierce de picardie* at the end.

A short, irregular, 'rather unpromising',[2] 'very odd' tune [3] of an 'a b a' shape, first improvised at the piano in the autumn of 1898, forms the basis of the *Variations on an Original Theme* for Orchestra, Op. 36, of 1899. On an inner page is inscribed 'Dedicated to my friends pictured within' and over the first page of the score is the word 'Enigma'. Lady Elgar thought that the composer was doing something that had never been done before—but it is not clear in what way:

---

[1] See Young, *op. cit.*, p. 275.

[2] See Buckley, *op. cit.*, p. 55.

[3] See Powell, *op. cit.*, p. 12.

Although Elgar originally mapped out eight bars for the middle major section and reduced it, the first part consists of the unusual number of six bars (followed by a double bar). Mozart's minuet, be it noted, starts with two three-bar phrases and not with the more conventional two or four bars. This theme is certainly stilted as it stands: a rest followed by two quavers and two crotchets alternating with a rest followed by two crotchets and two quavers for no less than twelve bars—and in the remaining four bars, in the middle, the same rhythmic pattern throughout:

♩ ♫ ×8

There follow fourteen variations with initials or nicknames to designate the composer's friends. In a letter to Jaeger of 24th October 1898, he said: 'I have sketched a set of Variations (orkestra) on an original theme . . . labelled 'em with the nick-names of my particular friends—*you* are Nimrod. That is to say I've written the variations each one to represent the mood of the "party" —I've liked to imagine the "party" writing the var: him (or her) self and have written what I think they wd. have written—if they were asses enough to compose.' In another letter to Jaeger [1] he said

[1] See *Musical Times*, October 1900.

he 'looked at the theme through the personality (as it were) of another Johnny': 'it's a quaint idea and the result is amusing to those behind the scenes and won't affect the hearer who "nose nuffin".' In fact in the programme note for the first performance on 19th June 1899 he stated that their idiosyncrasies 'need not have been mentioned publicly'. Dunhill says: 'Great musical works . . . often owe their existence to exterior influences with which the public has no concern. When a composer takes his prospective audience into his confidence . . . he creates, perhaps, an added zest in listening. But when he stops short of telling them the whole story . . . he starts tongues wagging.'[1]

Because of the many misleading comments arising from his tantalizing 'Enigma' subtitle, it has become necessary to subject his musical pictures to further scrutiny. His most important pronouncement, in the programme note, was: 'The enigma I will not explain—its "dark saying" must be left unguessed, and I warn you that the apparent connection between the variations and the theme is often of the slightest texture; further, through and over the whole set another and larger theme "goes", but is not played.' From this it can be seen that the problem must be divided into two parts. Referring to the Finale in a letter to Jaeger of 30th June 1899, Elgar crosses out the words, '1st theme' and substitutes, 'principal motive (Enigma)', so there is a hint that the enigma is attached in some way to the theme. As early as 1904 Buckley, without any obvious grounds, categorically stated that 'the theme is a counterpoint on some well-known melody', while Dunhill in 1938, again without any grounds, said that the 'larger Theme . . . only existed in the composer's mind'. It is important to notice carefully how Elgar's views on the original stimuli changed through the years; for this purpose I give overleaf a summary of what has been deduced or said on each movement.

[1] Thomas F. Dunhill, *Sir Edward Elgar* (1938), p. 83.

Elgar

Do = Mrs R. Powell (Dorabella), 1937
Du = T. F. Dunhill, 1938
E = Elgar (as above)
N = Ernest Newman, 1904
Y = Percy Young, 1954

I ('C.A.E.') *The Composer's Wife*

Alice, who became Elgar's pupil in 1886, had an instinctive faith that her husband-to-be was a genius. They were married in May 1889.

Alice did not literally help her husband with the composition (Do) but 'those who knew C.A.E. will understand this reference to one whose life was a romantic & delicate inspiration' (E).

II ('H.D.S.-P.') *Hew David Steuart-Powell*

Pianist in trio with Elgar and Basil Nevinson; his finger-loosening exercises were diatonic.

'His characteristic diatonic runs over the keys . . . here humorously travestied . . . chromatic beyond H.D.S.-P.'s liking' (E).

III ('R.B.T.') *Richard Baxter Townshend*

The story goes back to 1895 (Do) that he had to act, against his will, the part of an old man in which he used a high falsetto. An eccentric, he rode about Oxford on a tricycle with a bell continually ringing. His voice fascinated Mrs Elgar Blake as a child.

'. . . The low voice flying off occasionally into "soprano" timbre' (E).

IV ('W.M.B.') *William Meath Baker*

A Wagnerian. He liked to lay down the law. One of his sisters married the father of Dorabella

'. . . Read out the arrangements for the day and hurriedly left the music-room with an inadvertent

and the other married Richard Townshend.

bang of the door . . . some suggestions of the teasing attitude of the guests [figs. 13–14 in canon]' (E).

V ('R.P.A.') *Richard Penrose Arnold*

Son of the poet, Matthew Arnold, a 'gentleman of the old school' (Do).

'Whimsical & witty' (E).

VI ('Ysobel') *Isabel Fitton*

Viola-player who had to practise leaps across the strings. Very serious, sombre and contemplative (N).

Years afterwards, when conducting a performance of the work in Worcester, Elgar was astounded that Miss Fitton, despite 'Ysobel', still made the errors that he had sought to overcome (Y).

VII ('Troyte') *Arthur Troyte Griffith*

Not as noisy as this one-in-a-bar variation would suggest. Perhaps it represented an invigorating walk (N) over the Malvern Hills in blustery weather. He was a quiet man, a painter, designer and architect.

Mrs Elgar Blake reminded me that there were (friendly) arguments, her father being a strong Conservative and Troyte Griffith a very strong Liberal.

'The uncouth rhythm of the drums and lower strings was really suggested by some maladroit essays to play the pianoforte' (E), but 'I never heard E.E. try to make him play the piano' (Do) and 'it is impossible to believe that E. really meant what he said. . . . May we not believe that Elgar (like another famous composer) delighted to indulge in "leg-pulling" when people became over-inquisitive?' (Du).

VIII ('W.N.') *Winifred Norbury*

Winifred and her sister Florence lived at Sherridge, near Elgar's house, Birchwood. She met Troyte for the first time in March 1898. She had a trilly laugh which Elgar deliberately used to encourage.

'Really suggested by an eighteenth-century house' (E), the music is connected to the next variation but in fact Miss Norbury and Mr Jaeger only met on two or three occasions (Do).

Elgar

IX ('Nimrod') *August Johannes Jaeger*

Beethoven, Pf. Sonata, Op. 13.   Elgar. Notes that correspond to
  Adagio cantabile (transposed)   Beethoven are starred.

'I have omitted your outside manners & have only seen the good, lovable honest SOUL in the middle of you,' Elgar wrote on 13th March 1899 to Jaeger (German for Hunter, thus 'Nimrod'). His 'outside manner' was in fact amusing and almost racy (Do). This represents Elgar's gratitude to Jaeger who, when Elgar wanted to give up writing altogether, preached the example of Beethoven.

'No one could approach Beethoven at his best in slow movements (said Jaeger), a view with which I cordially concurred. . . . Jaeger was for years the dear friend, the valued adviser & the stern critic of many musicians beside the writer; his place has been occupied but never filled'. (E).

X ('Dorabella') *Dora Penny*

Probably subtitled Intermezzo because of its slight connection with the theme. Elgar first called Miss Penny 'Dorabella' in September 1898, explaining that it was a quotation from Mozart's *Così fan tutte*. She had a stammer.

Not in the least theatrical (Du); 'suggests a dance-like lightness' (E).

XI ('G.R.S.') *George Robertson Sinclair*

Dr Sinclair, organist of Hereford Cathedral from 1889, had the reputation of never playing a

'We jumped to the conclusion that this represented the musician's skill on the pedal-board of

wrong pedal note (evidence of E. C. Broadhurst given to the author). The scoring of bar 2 for bassoons (mf) and double basses (p) *without* cellos should make this obvious point. The addition of tuba (ff) two bars after fig. 50 gives the effect of an organist drawing a stop.

'G.R.S. will be no mystery to anyone who knows the names of the "Three Choir" organists' (N). Elgar started visiting him about 1896 and wrote in the Visitors' Book musical quotations called 'The Moods of Dan'. (Sir Percy Hull to Do, 13th June 1944.)

Sinclair died in 1917 and yet another so-called 'growl' appears in the String Quartet the following year (last movement: five bars before fig. 39). (See opposite column.) In any case at the same point in *King Olaf* the violins anticipate 'Dorabella' (not shown in vocal score).

his instrument, only to be corrected by the composer' (Du). (See also Maine, ii, p. 112.)

'The variation has nothing to do with organs or cathedrals, or, except remotely, with G.R.S. The first few bars were suggested by his great bulldog Dan (a well-known character) falling down the steep bank into the river Wye (bar 1); his paddling up stream to find a landing place (bars 2 & 3); and his rejoicing bark on landing (second half of bar 5). G.R.S. said, "Set that to music". I did; here it is' (E).

Dorabella had a 'growl' (bar 5) written into her vocal score of *King Olaf* ('watchdog', sc. 9) by Elgar in October 1896 (Do.). True, the full score of *King Olaf* has a similar viola motive, and again for 'foot print', so this *may* be taken as a touch of Dan. Tovey [1] asking 'Mr G.R.S. for his dog-licence' is just being wise after the event.

XII ('B.G.N.') *Basil Nevinson*

Cellist (see Var. II).

'A tribute to a very dear friend' (E).

XIII ('***') *Lady Mary Lygon*

Subtitled 'Romanza', the first sketches were marked 'L'. Elgar

'The drums suggest the distant throb of the engines of a liner over

---

[1] Sir Donald Tovey, *Essays in Musical Analysis*, vol. iv (1936).

intended to get Lady Mary's permission for the use of initials, but she was already on the high seas bound for Australia.

In the score the timpani roll is marked 'with side-drum sticks'. In fact, in June 1899, Charles Henderson of Richter's orchestra played with two coins. This pleased the composer and it is now always done that way.

which the clarinet quotes a phrase from Mendelssohn's "Calm Sea and Prosperous Voyage"' (E).

In 1905 Lady Mary Lygon was married to Major the Hon. Henry Forbes-Trefusis.

XIV ('E.D.U.') *Finale*

This is the composer himself, Edu, short for Eduard, being the name by which he was known to Alice. Elgar used to give a whistle to announce his return (four bars before fig. 73; also in ob. & fag. of Var. I) to Alice (Do).

'Written at a time when friends were dubious and generally discouraging ... the work is summed up in the triumphant, broad presentation of the theme in the major' (E).

A study of these double columns will reveal several inconsistencies, the grossest concerning 'Troyte' and 'G.R.S.'—both fast and noisy variations. If Dunhill had exercised his incredulity about the latter rather than about the former, we might have had confirmation of a vital link in the mystery. When Elgar specifically says 'G.R.S.' has 'nothing to do with organs or cathedrals' he sounds like the boy who said he did *not* throw the little girl's hat out of the window. Has he something to hide? Did Elgar and his wife constantly divert attention from the truth? It was Sir Jack Westrup who first suggested that the original form of the theme was possibly such a sequence of notes as is presented in 'G.R.S.' [1] Indeed how many classical masters would start with a theme in which rests in the melody line come at the beginning of bars? Only,

[1] Professor J. A. Westrup, 'Elgar's Enigma', *Proceedings of the Royal Musical Association*, 23rd April 1960.

perhaps, if one were thinking as a violinist, as Elgar would, but even the Bach *Chaconne* for unaccompanied violin does not exploit this across-the-strings technique in the theme. Surely the theme, as it stands, is more like a variation. Here are examples from other composers for comparison:

Composer and Title	Number of Variations	First Use of Rests at Beginning of Bar
Purcell		
Grand Dance (*King Arthur*)	Theme & 15	Var. 8 = ♩ ♩ ♩	×6
Bach		
Organ Passacaglia	Theme & 20	Var. 1 = ♩ ♩ ♪ ♪	
Mozart		
Sonata in A ma, K.331	Theme & 6	Var. 4 = ♪ ♫ ♫♪	
Beethoven		
32 Variations	Theme & 32	Theme = ♩ ♩.. ♪ (first bar)
Diabelli Variations	Theme & 33	Var. 2 = ♪ ♪ ♪ ♪ ♪ ♪	×32
Eroica Symphony	Theme & 8	None
Schumann		
Études Symphoniques	Theme & 12	None (Appendix 4 has some)
Brahms		
Symphony No. 4	Theme & 30	Var. 1 = ♩ ♩ ♩	×8

From this random list only Beethoven once seems to start the theme with a rest (in the *32 Variations*) and that for only one bar.

CHAPTER VIII

THE ENIGMA: A SOLUTION

WHEN we consider that more than seventy fruitless years have passed, it may seem surprising that it should now be possible to offer a solution to the enigma—and indeed to both parts. For help with the first part, unravelling the enigma's 'dark saying', I am much indebted to the Rt Rev. John Richards, Bishop of St Davids.

Elgar was a Roman Catholic, helped his father as organist and was familiar with the language of the Roman Mass. Were not his friends to see themselves through these variations as in the Vulgate version of I. Cor. xiii. 12: 'Videmus nunc per speculum in aenigmate',[1] words which come in the Quinquagesima Mass in the Epistle?[2] The last word is from the Greek αἴνιγμα, which is translated in the Revised Version margin as 'in a riddle'. The passage in the Authorized Version is: 'For now we see through a glass, darkly; but then face to face: now I know in part; but then shall I know even as also I am known.' Elgar gave a clue by his use of the word 'dark', in the meaning of obscure, literally or figura‑ tively. The *New English Bible* has: 'Now we see only puzzling reflections in a mirror, but then we shall see face to face. My knowledge now is partial; then it will be whole, like God's knowledge of me.' For further confirmation of how Elgar felt about himself—his reaching maturity as a composer but massive lack of

[1] Βλέπομεν γὰρ ἄρτι δι'ἐσόπτρου ἐν αἰνίγματι, τότε δέ πρόσωπον πρὸς πρόσωπον· ἄρτι γινώσκω ἐκ μέρους, τότε δὲ ἐπιγνώσομαι καθὼς καὶ ἐπεγνώσθην.

[2] Elgar knew his Vulgate (letter of 11th April 1902 to Jaeger) and his liturgy (ditto, 1st March 1903); he quoted Titus I. 12 (ditto, 22nd March 1903).

recognition—we may read the verses of the Bible before and after verse 12:

> 11. When I was a child, my speech, my outlook, and my thoughts were all childish. When I grew up, I had finished with childish[1] things.
>
> 13. In a word, there are three things that last for ever; faith, hope, and love; but the greatest of them all is love.

If the above solution is correct, Elgar's remark of November 1899 to Dorabella fits into place: 'Haven't you guessed it yet? Try again.' 'Are you quite sure I know it?' 'Quite.' And on another occasion: 'Well I'm surprised. I thought you of all people would guess it.'[2] This could now be interpreted as meaning that the daughter of a clergyman (Dorabella's father was Rector of St Peter's Collegiate Church, Wolverhampton, from 1895) should know her Bible.

Elgar orchestrated the work during early February (the autograph bears the inscription: 'Ended Feb. 19th 1899'). In a letter of this date to Jaeger he calls it just *Variations*, and on another occasion 'symphonic variations'; the word 'enigma' is not used until May, so it seems. The score was sent to Richter's manager on 21st February[3] and the great conductor's acceptance of it proved to be a turning-point in Elgar's career.

In 1899 Quinquagesima Sunday fell on February 12th. So the reading of I. Cor. xiii must have been in the composer's mind during the final week's scoring. The Bishop adds, for the thought underlying the *Variations*, that the previous chapter, I. Cor. xii, has as its main theme 'Diversity in Unity': one spirit, but a diversity of gifts; one body, but a diversity of limbs; one Lord, but a diversity of ministries. Love alone can maintain the diversity in true unity. And I. Cor. xiii is a chapter divided into thirteen verses: an interesting coincidence when one thinks of the thirteen friends 'pictured within' the *Variations*. According to Mrs Elgar

---

[1] In a letter of 4th July 1901 to Jaeger Elgar refers to Gerontius's 'memory (remembrance) of the soul—an utter childish (childlike) peace'.

[2] Powell, *op. cit.*, p. 119.

[3] Young, *op. cit.*, p. 87; McVeagh, *op. cit.*, p. 27.

Blake,[1] her mother's diary for Sunday 12th February 1899 has the entry: 'E. to S. Joseph's.' Elgar, therefore, did go to Mass that day —at the nearest Roman Catholic church in Malvern. So, from Quinquagesima 1899, Elgar and his thirteen friends were to see each other in a new way.

We may now turn to the second and harder part of the problem: the larger theme that 'goes'. If your friend is a viola player or a cellist, you are free to pay gracious tribute to his playing, but if an organist you are not? Why not? Is Elgar playing an extravagant confidence trick on us? Or is he trying to divert our attention? I am compelled at last to the view that he is trying to take our minds away from 'G.R.S.' The bulldog may never have put a paw wrong in the Wye. The fact is that E. C. Broadhurst was assistant to Sinclair from 1892 to 1896 and, like his master, never played a wrong pedal note. I myself was a pupil of Broadhurst and can vouch for the fact that both players were proud of their pedalling. The Bach Gesellschaft edition was available in the mid-nineteenth century and both Sinclair and Elgar were enthusiasts. Elgar presented the complete edition to Birmingham University in 1905. Three works of Bach, all in G minor, anticipate much of Elgar's style: the chorale at the end of the motet, *Komm, Jesu, komm* (see the Angel's Alleluia in *Gerontius,* after fig. 12); the chorale variations for organ on *Sei gegrüsset,* where ten out of eleven movements end with a *tierce de Picardie*; and the unfinished pedal *Exercitium* for organ:

Ex. 3

where most of the intervals of 'G.R.S.', bar 2, can be noticed (note also the orchestration):

Ex. 4

---

[1] Letter of 26th April 1969.

The Enigma: a Solution

Elgar did not like to be told that his music was like anyone else's. Dorabella had her head snapped off more than once;[1] so did Jaeger and others. To mention Bach to him as someone from whom he 'cribbed' would have produced either a peppery outburst or a hurt withdrawal—or a cover-up in the form of a puzzle, so that he could laugh at his friends' failure to solve it.

It is unnecessary to try to fit in such tunes as 'Home, Sweet Home', 'Ta-ra-ra-boom-de-ay', 'Auld Lang Syne'[2] or Chopin's G minor Nocturne; all have been suggested, but their 'greatness' must be questioned.[3] Elgar was familiar with Wales; and in the traditional art of *penillion* singing a counterpoint of *words* and music is fitted to a harp air *after* the latter has started. The opening six-bar phrase followed by an apparently redundant double-bar would lend itself admirably to this treatment,[4] which none of the many ingenious contrapuntists has yet tried. However this also seems to be a dead end. I think it best to say simply that Bach was the inspiration behind the theme of the *Variations*, not as the writer of exact counterpoint but as a great and powerful imaginative writer whom Elgar admired probably more than any other composer (he did, after all, travel more than 150 miles from Düsseldorf in May 1902 to visit Bach's birthplace). Here, surely, is the greater *canto fermo* that 'goes' with Elgar's music which, on its own, starts as a variation.

Mrs Elgar Blake wrote to me on 7th July 1969 after reading the above, to say that she found it 'very interesting and a perfectly original point of view, not, so far as I know, put forward by anyone else. And most ingenious—I can't see *why* it could not be the answer, though I fear we shall none of us ever know for certain'.

[1] Powell, *op. cit.,* p. 52.

[2] Roger Fiske pursues this one in 'The Enigma: a solution' (*Musical Times*, November 1969, p. 1124) and confirms that Elgar sometimes intentionally misled.

[3] Elgar said, '*No. Auld Lang Syne* won't do. E.E.' on a postcard to Fox Strangways's friend, Dyneley Hussey, in 1929 (*Music and Letters*, January 1935).

[4] See Ian Parrott, *The Enigma : A New Slant* (Worcester, 1968).

CHAPTER IX

THE GREAT ORATORIOS

'I HAVE not seen or heard anything since "Parsifal" that has stirred me and spoken to me with the trumpet tongue of genius as has this part of your latest, and by far greatest work,' wrote Jaeger in May 1900. 'I except, perhaps, the Pathetic Symphony,[1] although that is but worldly, pessimistic, depressing, whereas your wonderful music is inexpressibly and wonderfully elevating, "aloof", mystic, and heart-moving, as by the force of a great compassion.' Thus, a fortnight before its completion, did Jaeger appreciate the quality of *The Dream of Gerontius*. In the centenary edition of the *Musical Times* (June 1957) at least five out of twenty-one distinguished contributors put *Gerontius* at the top of their list of masterpieces (with *Falstaff* the favourite in second place), while Miss McVeagh [2] categorically calls it his greatest work. Future generations may not agree. Writing to Jaeger in August, Elgar said he imagined Gerontius as a sinner, a worldly man and so he did not fill '*his* part with Church tunes & rubbish but a good, healthy full-blooded romantic, remembered worldliness'. 'It is,' he imagined, 'much more difficult to tear one's self away from a well to do world than from a cloister': and thus he characterized Gerontius in the music.

Maine thought that the average reader in the thirties would consider it as either an 'incomprehensible exposition of dogma or else as a Jesuitical attempt to make him swallow a theological pill hidden in the jam of a human story'.[3] Now, another thirty years on, much of the theology has fallen away, leaving only the music.

---

[1] The reference to Tchaikovsky is omitted in Kennedy, *op. cit.*, p. 79.
[2] *Op. cit.*, p. 129.
[3] *Op. cit.*, vol. ii, p. 37.

The Great Oratorios

Cardinal Newman's verses were selected with much care and understanding by the composer. An interesting comparison between the treatment of death and judgment by two Catholics is given by Norman Suckling when writing of Fauré's *Requiem* of 1887.[1] In Fauré there is passionless peace, ending in Paradise; while in Elgar there is the torment of the composer as well as of the subject. Much of *Gerontius* is like the Pathetic Symphony (introduced to Hereford by Sinclair in 1897): the opening theme; the wild exultation; the snarling trombones; the demons; and the final resignation, although this last is musically perhaps more like something between Wagner's 'Liebestod' in *Tristan* and the 'Good Friday Music' in *Parsifal*. And the composer thinks of instruments before voices. Even Walford Davies (*Radio Times*, 16th March 1934) says, in characteristic vein: 'Listen intently to the instruments rather than to the voices'—something that the general public is usually loath to do.

The opening bars have an awe-inspiring solemnity, but I feel a certain unease at the appearance of the fourth motive (at fig. 4), labelled by Jaeger in his complete Analytical Notes as 'the weary, troubled sleep of a sick man'. All the themes in the Prelude are striking and varied, but this one seems to have been designed for some languid secular occasion, where a *habanera* may have been half-abandoned. Incidentally, the now traditional silent pauses which halt the full orchestra so dramatically in the Prelude between figs. 9 and 10 were not in the original sketches. The treatment of the solo voice is fully Italianate. The composer even wrote two syllables to one note, as follows:

Ex. 5

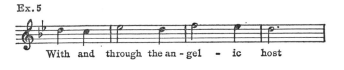

With and through the an - gel - ic host

[1] N. Suckling, *Fauré* (1946), pp. 175–6.

This was later printed as 'th'angelic'. In the first half, Gerontius, still alive, is guided towards his God. The chorus, his 'assistants' or, in the German edition, 'Freunde', produce the first wholly Elgarian sound with their Kyrie eleison (fig. 29). This is a motive which makes a magical reappearance (Part II, fig, 115) when the soul of Gerontius, to the accompaniment of harp, bass drum and lower strings and sustained organ, marked *pppp*, goes before its Judge.

In the introduction to Part II a feeling of other worldliness is achieved by *legato* strings; the conservative but discerning Professor Kitson says that 'the consecutives, i.e. the octaves in bar 5, actually provide the means of suggesting the conditions of a soul wandering in space'.[1] The soul 'hears' the sound of singing, though he cannot 'rightly say Whether I hear or touch or taste the tones'. First appearing in 5/8 time in the orchestra three bars before fig. 11, this theme becomes the lovely and later impassioned 'Alleluia' of the Angel, underlined in the bass three octaves below. The soul passes demons, 'Low born clods of brute earth', who make a terrifying ironic din with clanging orchestra, and then angelicals who sing another memorable Elgar melody, 'Praise to the Holiest' (fig. 61). Considerable momentum is built up, spoilt momentarily by a Gounod like chromaticism for 'O loving wisdom of our God' (fig. 75); there is nothing else in all of Elgar's works quite like this long pounding episode, culminating in a paean of praise (ending at fig. 101). The Angel of the Agony leads the soul to God for a short glimpse, where Elgar instructs every instrument for one moment to exert its fullest force (fig. 120). Finally a half chorus, a double chorus and the Angel bring the work to an end with something approaching the serenity of Fauré, though it is the peace after torment and the passion of someone who has attempted to solve the riddle of death.

I have referred above (Chapter II) to the solemn opening of *The Apostles*, which immediately proclaims a new and compelling musical language. For Edmund Rubbra this work was 'a major

---

[1] C. H. Kitson, *The Evolution of Harmony* (1914), p. 452.

THE BIRTHPLACE AT BROADHEATH, where Elgar lived for two and a half years.

BRINKWELLS, near Fittleworth, Sussex (before being rethatched in 1967), where the chamber music was written, 1918–19.

Sketches by Elizabeth Parrott

A FAMILY GROUP, WHEN EDWARD ELGAR WAS ABOUT
TWENTY-ONE.
Left to right: *back* Dot, Frank, Polly
front Lucy, Edward

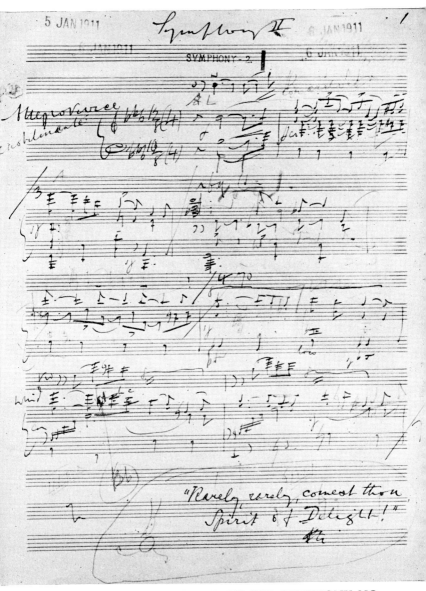

THE FIRST PAGE OF THE SKETCH FOR SYMPHONY NO. 2.

THE WAND OF YOUTH. A Faery Fantasy, rewritten by Winifred Barrows with Elgar's approval and performed in 1930, and again in 1957, by Lawnside School, Malvern.

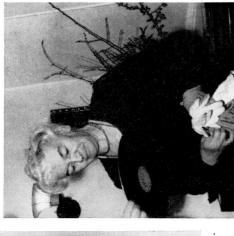

DR G. R. SINCLAIR WITH HIS
BULLDOG, DAN.

WINIFRED NORBURY, 1923.

'DORABELLA'
(MRS R. POWELL), 1936.

THREE FRIENDS 'PICTURED WITHIN'

197

EXAMPLE 5*b*

THE SECOND SUBJECT FOR THE FIRST MOVEMENT OF THE
UNFINISHED SYMPHONY NO. 3.

ELGAR in 1922.

SIR EDWARD ELGAR CONDUCTING IN THE H.M.V. RECORDING
LABORATORY. ABOUT 1915.

experience',[1] but only by a minority is it still considered one of the greatest. 'It has long been my wish,' wrote the composer as a preface to the score, 'to compose an oratorio which should embody the Calling of the Apostles, their Teaching (schooling) and their Mission, culminating in the establishment of the Church among the Gentiles'. With his considerable knowledge of the Bible and with much interest in theology at the time, Elgar was ready to compile his own text. The music from the dawn, with shofar and integrated ancient Hebrew melody, to the end of the first section is powerful. Observe how the unaccompanied 'Mission' music at fig. 3 is similar to but stronger than the passage at fig. 51 in the *Coronation Ode*. 'By the Wayside', with the Beatitudes, is more gentle, somewhat in the manner of Walford Davies (at that time a composer to be reckoned with). The third section, 'By the Sea of Galilee', combines various elements with considerable imagination: Mary Magdalene and her memories (chorus: 'Let us fill ourselves with costly wine') and a great tempest (chorus: 'He walketh on the waters'). Mary Magdalene, a genuinely repentant sinner, takes her place as a soloist beside Peter and the other disciples, and her characteristic music is added to theirs. In Caesarea Philippi they are joined by the Virgin Mary. Criticisms by Jaeger of this part were all ignored by the composer: the phrase 'ye shall lie down' (vocal score, p. 83) was like 'God save the King'; 'And I will give you the keys of the kingdom of heaven' (p. 102) was 'too jolly'; and 'Turn you to the stronghold' (p. 109) was 'crude'. This last indictment hurt Elgar enough for it to stay in his mind; often he joked to Jaeger about it, signing himself 'Crood' or 'Cruuuuuuud'.

Almost certainly the finest single episode is the first of Part II, 'The Betrayal'. Not only is Judas a strongly drawn character, but the use of the chorus (within the Temple) has a very compelling effect, as the drama, from the pieces of silver to his suicide, unfolds. Note the hard silvery effect of the 'price of blood', with cymbals, triangle, glockenspiel and, especially macabre, organ manual

[1] *Musical Times*, June 1957.

triplets with two, four and sixteen foot stops. After the Crucifixion and Ascension a beautiful amalgam of angels singing Alleluias with earthly chorus and soloists, including a touch of 'Is it nothing to you?' in the eighteenth section of Stainer's *Crucifixion* (1887) at 'They mocked Him' (2 bars before fig. 227), brings the oratorio to an end.

The intention, however, is that *The Kingdom* should be performed on the following evening. Here the apostles, filled with zeal, go out into the world to preach, and the composer's music has the same urgency and exaltation, particularly in the optimistic opening Prelude, which involves the *nota cambiata* plainsong 'Constitues eos', used as a motive representing the apostles. Many themes from the other oratorio reappear and sometimes develop. The organ is often used in its own right as an orchestral instrument with its own characteristics and not as a continuo or mere stiffener. At fig. 6 appears the dignified 'New Faith' motive, serenely Elgarian with its rising sequences and diatonic discords. The language of the second oratorio is ripe—unmistakably characteristic is the music for the two Marys, 'At the Beautiful Gate', or 'the tongues parting asunder, like a fire' (fig. 78) at Pentecost, when the composer seems himself filled with the Holy Spirit—but the structure is looser. The arrest of the apostles gives way to one of Elgar's greatest single compositions: the soliloquy for the Virgin Mary, 'The sun goeth down'. Hebrew melodies are again woven into the texture [1]; to Adela Schuster he wrote on 17th March 1933, 'The Jews have always been my best and kindest friends'. If he had written nothing else, this aria would be memorable in its original harmony, subtle changes of tempo and in its fastidious orchestration. Sir Adrian Boult has rated *The Kingdom* higher than *Gerontius*. 'It maintains throughout,' he says, 'a stream of glorious music,' [2] and in April 1969 he made for E.M.I. the first complete recording. The last section represents the Fellowship in the Upper Room, and includes the insertion of the Lord's Prayer; one

[1] Jaeger, Analytical Notes (1906), p. 39.
[2] See Alec Robertson, *Radio Times*, 31st July 1969, p. 35.

cannot help wondering whether the confidence of the opening has slipped a little in this serene ending. Elgar did not complete a third oratorio for the trilogy. He probably would have called it not 'The Judgement', but 'The Saints'.[1] The last theme he ever wrote, however, was called 'The Judgement' and as he gave it to W. H. Reed, he said, 'This is the end, Billy'.

[1] Young, *op. cit.*, p. 255.

CHAPTER X

MISCELLANEOUS INSTRUMENTAL WORKS

ELGAR was first and foremost an instrumental composer, even when he used the human voice. Thanks to his early practical experience, he soon outstripped all his contemporaries in his technique even before a personal style had evolved. The almost wholly unoriginal *Sursum Corda*, Op. 11, of 1894, with its almost sanctimoniously complacent and expected phrases, is yet extremely carefully orchestrated for the combination of two trumpets, four horns, three trombones, tuba, timpani, organ and strings. The organ is an integral part but there is no sign as yet of the composer using it in his constant efforts to produce a more sonorous bass line. The treatment of the strings is already masterly and almost every note is carefully marked with phrasing, bowing, accents, *tenuto*, fingering, the string to be used, and so on. As he said later to Reed,[1] any sets of notes without nuances, accents or stress marks, etc., were 'naked' and the passage 'tame'. It may be added that this work is not improved in Max Leistner's ingenious transcription for piano, published in 1901, in which the introduction is reduced, while five extra bars are gratuitously inserted in the middle and the Gounod-like barley-sugar at the end is drawn out by a further eight bars. Elgar was not the victim when, while adding parts for Heinrich Esser's transcription for orchestra of Bach's *Toccata* in F major,[2] he restored the original strong ending in place of an outrageous coda.

The composer had already completed a good deal of miscellaneous orchestral composition, mostly without more than a flair for pulling off an effective trifle, and he continued thus. 'Contrasts: The Gavotte A.D. 1700 and 1900', the third of *Three Pieces for Small Orchestra*, Op. 10 (some dating back to 1882), is typical.

[1] *Elgar as I knew him*, p. 141.
[2] Young says D minor (*op. cit.*, p. 424).

One of his early pieces with real charm and delicacy as well as popularity was *Salut d'Amour*, Op. 12, which, although available in many forms, is worth looking at again in score for the impeccable placing of notes. It was dismissed by Walker as 'West-End drawing-room' music.[1] Also popular were *Chanson de Nuit* and *Chanson de Matin*, Op. 15, No. 1 and No. 2, of 1897 and 1899 respectively, violin and piano pieces later arranged for orchestra.[2]

Since they made effective use of very early material, the two *Wand of Youth* suites may be considered at this stage, although they were not published until 1907 and 1908. Here is shown Elgar's great skill in getting 'out of himself' in order to entertain rather than to uplift. Both suites are subtitled 'Music to a child's play' and this indicates the intention though no actual play is provided. A 'Faery Fantasy' to the music, rewritten by Winifred Barrows with Elgar's permission, was performed at Lawnside School, Malvern, in 1930. Elgar himself wrote some 'notes':

> Some small grievances occasioned by the imaginary despotic rule of my father and mother (The Two Old People) led to the devising of 'The Wand of Youth'. By means of a stage-allegory—which was never wholly completed—it was proposed to show that children were not properly understood.

> The scene was a Woodland Glade, intersected by a brook; the hither side of this was our fairyland; beyond, small and distant, was the ordinary life which we forgot as often as possible. The characters on crossing the stream, entered fairyland and were transfigured. The Old People were lured over the bridge by the 'Moths and Butterflies' and the 'Little Bells', but these devices did not please; the Old People were restive and failed to develop that fairy feeling necessary for their well-being. While fresh devices were making 'The Fairy Pipers' charmed them to sleep; this sleep was accompanied by 'The Slumber Scene'. To awaken the Old People glittering lights were flashed in their eyes by means of 'Sun Dance'. Other episodes—'The Fountain Dance', etc., whose character can be deduced from the titles, followed, and the whole concluded with the March.
>
> March 1929.

[1] Ernest Walker, *A History of Music in England* (1907), p. 304.
[2] These are listed by Young in the reverse order.

These 'notes', found in the school album at Lawnside, were printed when *The Wand of Youth* music was recorded. Elgar had hoped to conduct the reconstructed play but was prevented by illness. How gaily this early carefree music trips along! And what a characteristic clarinet tune appears in the 'Serenade', and how vividly pictorial are the 'Fairies and Giants' (first sketched when the composer was only ten and thus preceding Tchaikovsky's *Nutcracker* music of 1892 in composition if not in orchestration) of the first suite! Not until the second subject of 'The Little Bells' in the second suite does the introspective composer begin to dominate. In his youth Elgar must have been moved to compassion by the sight of a chained bear shuffling along, for the onomatopoeia of percussion in 'The Tame Bear' is instinctively right, matching the pathos of the music, as is the similar clanking of 'The Wagon Passes' in the later *Nursery Suite*; the latter was, incidentally, the favourite movement, when recorded in 1931, of the Duke and Duchess of York and their daughters, the Princesses Elizabeth and Margaret. Deriving seemingly from one of Mussorgsky's *Pictures at an Exhibition*, it has the flavour of an old Worcestershire carter whistling a tune on his way through Broadheath.[1] 'The Tame Bear', however, takes one more to the Kremlin square of *Boris*.

Elgar's earliest concert overture of substance was *Froissart*, Op. 19. Full of youthful vigour, with a quotation from Keats, 'When Chivalry lifted her lance up on high', at the head of the score, it is now seen to be somewhat derivative, though the scoring is assured, with its subtle placing of string parts and beautiful distribution of wind lines. Not for nothing had the young composer started making his visits to Germany. More modest in conception but more lasting has proved the *Serenade* for string orchestra, Op. 20, in which the authentic voice of the composer can be heard, especially in the slow movement.

Separate consideration is given in this book to the *Enigma Variations* (see Chapter VII). In addition to the five extrovert *Pomp*

----

[1] See Reed, *Elgar*, p. 2.

and Circumstance military marches (preceded by the bright but formal *Imperial March* of 1897) there is a splendid piece in the same tradition, the concert overture *Cockaigne*, with an abundance of good tunes descriptive of London Town—the soldiers, the urchins, the lovers, the Salvation Army, the churches—a London, said Edwin Evans, on the threshold of that period of social splendour which we know as Edwardian.[1] Music of Elgar's prime includes also the delicate *Dream Children* and the boisterous, episodic *Introduction and Allegro* for string quartet and string orchestra.

Nothing could be more typical of the composer at the beginning of his 'second period' than the exuberant first subject of the latter. Equally typical is the speed with which it gives way to the dreamy second subject (six bars after fig. 2), inspired first by the sound of distant Welsh voices at Ynys Lochtyn in Cardiganshire (see Chapter III). John Horton has suggested the Welsh folk tune *Bugeilio'r gwenith gwyn*,[2] but the more likely theme, as already stated, is *Hen Wlad Fy Nhadau*, though members of the Welsh Folk Song Society continue to imagine that they hear other tunes. What transforms the 'Welsh' tune, in any case, is the slide-slipping accompaniment, which develops four bars after fig. 3; compare it with the lovely subsidiary idea in *Cockaigne* five bars before fig. 5. It is easy to say that this great work for string quartet and string orchestra derives from the old *concerto grosso*, but in fact this is what Elgar hardly ever lets it do: there is never a true alternation of soloists and *ripieno* players. Take, for example, the appearance of the quartet at fig. 3. They are not playing on their own (as they might at first imagine), their lines being blurred by a fuzzy touching-up of odd notes on the orchestral violas and the addition of double basses. Elgar never leaves his parts clear, as a classical composer would (compare his scoring of Handel's Overture in D minor with Handel's own orchestral writing). Even when writing a fugue, as he does in the middle of the present work, the whole quartet is used at the unison to reinforce the bass line for two beats

[1] Pocket score note.
[2] 'Two Possible Elgar Allusions', *Musical Times*, August 1960.

(four bars before fig. 20). Another curious idea completes the material of this work: the throbbing syncopated chords at fig. 10, which seem to have something Spanish about them—more over-heard music, perhaps, on a hot evening in a sunnier clime?[1]

Elgar's favourite 'sunnier clime' was in fact Italy, though one feels at the beginning of the concert overture *In the South* (*Alassio*) that he had stopped short in Munich, since the first subject is so strongly Straussian. The most arresting idea is that associated with the past might of Imperial Rome—the historic past often impressed him more than the present—though there is a gentle *canto popolare* too. This sort of 'folk-tune' atmosphere, incidentally, was recap-tured in October 1905 with one of his quite distinguished short piano pieces, *In Smyrna*.

Short works worthy of note—and revival—are the *Romance* for bassoon and orchestra of 1910 and the sadly beautiful *Sospiri* of 1914. Not only is the latter in Elgar's most mature manner but in some ways it breaks the new ground that Bloch was on, with its dissonances moving not by step but by thirds (see, for example, the third bar) and a melodic line not only with sevenths but with agonized ninths (see bar before fig. 3).

The 'symphonic study' *Falstaff*, on which the composer had been working for more than ten years, was first performed at the Leeds Festival in 1913. For it Elgar published his own 'analytical notes', and in some ways he demanded more imagination from the listener than was reasonable. His own knowledge of Shakespeare was encyclopaedic (see Chapter III) and his delineation of the central figures is sumptuous, beautifully set off by two delicately nostalgic 'interludes' or 'dream-pictures', in which Jack Falstaff reminisces about his youth. The changing and deteriorating rela-tionship between Falstaff and Henry V is treated deftly and the metamorphosis of themes (e.g. from fig. 96 to fig. 103) is often very subtle. The theme for Falstaff starts, rightly, to swagger—gay, easy, corpulent—and later becomes gargantuan. The theme for the King

[1] Could Bartók ever have heard this? See 'Concerto for Orchestra', II, fig. 116 foll.

while still a prince is regal: in fact it seems to be a youthful relation of King Mark:

Ex.6
(a) Wagner, *Tristan.* 'King Mark'
  Lento moderato

Bass Cl.*p*

(b) Elgar, *Falstaff.* 'Prince Henry' second phrase
  Allegro

Tutti *ff*

The work as a whole is bubbling over with tunes and there is much 'working out' of them though, as Miss McVeagh notes, it is often more fugal than symphonic.[1] There is indeed some amusing fuguing at fig. 44: but the treatment is also to some extent symphonic. For example, when Falstaff leads his 'scarecrow army' to battle, there is a shuttle-cocking of material from bass to treble (fig. 93) somewhat like the development section of the first movement of his early valued model: Mozart's G Minor Symphony. As is frequent in Elgar, the brash new sounds (the alternating chromaticisms at fig. 19 or the clashing brass at fig. 83) are now less memorable than such things as the diatonic theme at fig. 32—which Elgar called 'cheerful out-of-doors ambling'. After those personal outpourings, the great oratorios, the symphonies, and the Violin Concerto, *Falstaff* appears somewhat detached, and yet this work is autobiographical, from the optimistic loyalty expressed in the opening to the sad repudiation at the end. The 'loyalty-motive' (fig. 119) appears, in fact, as a sketch labelled 'Farewell to the Hut', July 1913, *espressivo*, and 'Written on Thursday after you left and

[1] *Op. cit.,* p. 174.

now Good night. E.E.' (Lord Northampton and Julia Worthington had died in the previous month and there is no doubt that Elgar
was in solemn mood.) To show whether one is in Eastcheap,
Gadshill, the Boar's Head, Westminster Abbey, or Gloucester-
shire, etc., and who are present, the Hostess, Doll Tearsheet, Pistol,
etc., would it not be good to perform Elgar's *Falstaff* to a film some
time?

The orchestration of Hubert Parry's *Jerusalem* dates from the
time of the Leeds Festival of 1922, when the first half of one
concert was devoted to Parry's music.[1] It was used again by Sir
Hugh Allen, to whom it was dedicated, and it was performed
under Elgar's baton at the Aberystwyth Festival of 1923, with
Walford Davies trying to add to the noise by playing an un-
authorized piano duet, with the lid open, with Charles Clements.
The scoring does not ask for piano, but characteristic use is made
of the organ, the basses sometimes have ♫♩♫ instead of ♩,
so as to keep pressing out the tone, and in the second verse 'Bring me
my spear' has elaborate figuration for strings and sharp ejacula-
tions for brass. Altogether it is a worthy example of what Elgar
could do but Parry could not: orchestrate.

[1] See letter from Sir Jack Westrup in the *Musical Times*, October 1969.

CHAPTER XI

INCIDENTAL MUSIC, SONGS AND PART-SONGS

W. B. YEATS was not given to flattering musicians. In fact he usually objected strongly to music being associated in any way with his poetry. Nevertheless, he said of Elgar's incidental music to *Grania and Diarmid* (1901), a play by himself and George Moore, that it was 'wonderful in its heroic melancholy'. There is incidental music and a fine Funeral March as well as a lovely song for the first act; all of them show character. After this one has to wade a long way through a number of trivial and uninspired occasional pieces, searching in vain for the true Elgar. One of these, the masque *The Crown of India*, dates from the composer's ripest period, 1912, but it contains little of value. The sumptuous orchestration may deceive some into feeling that there is originality in, say, the 'March of the Mogul Emperors'; in fact there is only a tremendous technique. The war-time music was stirring at the time. The effect of *Carillon* in 1914, when Germany invaded Belgium, was like the 'brandishing of a sword'.[1] Of the later works most are unimportant: *The Fringes of the Fleet* and the ballet *The Sanguine Fan*, both of 1917, the music to a production of *King Arthur*, 1923, the *Pageant of Empire* for the 1924 Wembley Exhibition, the music for *Beau Brummel*, 1928. There is one exception: most of the music which he lavished on a comparatively unworthy play in 1915 has a lightness and charm which are wholly delightful. This was for the fanciful children's play *The Starlight Express* by Violet Pearn, based on a book by Algernon Blackwood. There is at least one waltz song with a technique and imagination worthy of the Johann Strauss family: 'The Blue-Eyes Fairy'. Some other movements such as the 'Dance of the Pleiades' go through the

[1] Maine, *op. cit.*, vol. i, p. 204.

motions of contemporary light opera and musical comedy, and the
'Sunrise Song' takes one back to Sherridge, where one can see
W.N. looking out of the window. The strongest effect comes with
a quotation from the *Wand of Youth*, 'Little Bells', which is used
throughout the play as a leading motive and is worked into and
developed in the Finale with real gusto and even put alongside
'The First Nowell'. Clearly an escape to the stars with children
released some creative energy in Elgar, which other topics failed
to do, although *Carillon* the previous year had produced a strong
ostinato figure.

Although he had thought of opera on many occasions, he
finally got down to the idea too late. He was already a sick man
when Bernard Shaw politely refused to be his librettist and passed
him on to Sir Barry Jackson. Jackson's first reaction [1] was astonish‑
ment that Elgar should want to take not one of Ben Jonson's better‑
known plays, but *The Devil is an Ass*, which he thought quite
moribund. 'Nothing,' he said at first, 'could be done with it.'
Later, prodded by the enthusiastic Elgar, he found a 'splendid
story for an opera . . . fined down to the uttermost dramatic limits
in my version', after which Elgar added incidents and complica‑
tions over which they fought, Barry Jackson with his vast stage
experience and Elgar perhaps not so practical. The opera project,
called *The Spanish Lady*—again a pull towards Spain—did not
come to fruition, although much detailed planning went on [2] (see
page 78).

Writing bitterly to Jaeger after the first and unsuccessful per‑
formance of *Gerontius*, Elgar said (12th October 1900): 'All my
best friends including the highest thinkers only made one remark
during my "exaltation": now you must write a few popular songs
. . . that will make up for this.' As is often the case, the worst music
may sometimes make more money and, by trying to carry out his
friends' advice, Elgar put his name to some very feeble, dated
rubbish of which we can now only feel ashamed. When on

[1] See Reed, *Elgar as I knew him*, p. 90.
[2] Young, *op. cit.*, pp. 360–75.

occasion he rises above the trivialities of fashion he seems to copy previous song-writers: in 'In the Dawn' it is Schumann and Schubert; in 'Is She not Passing Fair?' it is Brahms; and so on. This is not the stuff of which a new school of British song-writing is made. In fact it was left to composers like Peter Warlock to establish this with a truly new and original approach in the twenties.

One song, however, stands out. Significantly it was originally an instrumental item. The trio tune of the first *Pomp and Circumstance* march (1901) became in the following year 'Land of Hope and Glory' in the *Coronation Ode*. The splendid broad lines, which grew out of Elgar's love of the pageantry associated with imperial Britain, were split up with many repeated notes to accommodate A. C. Benson's words. A glance at the following sample will show how this was done and it will be seen further that the general public, who have taken the tune to their hearts, do not now in fact follow Elgar's rhythmic pattern in many places.

Ex.7

Older readers must have regretted the announcement in *The Times* of 6th June 1969 that 'Rule, Britannia' and 'Land of Hope and Glory', following the death of Sargent in 1967, were to be dropped from their traditional position on the last night of the London 'Proms'. The B.B.C. relented a month later, however, after a storm of protests from all sides, and the two patriotic songs were restored once more.

Returning to the minims of the original, Elgar arranged the tune himself for cello and piano: a 'Duet for two nice people by another (nice) Person, op. x' and at the end, 'Repeat ad infinitum, ad nauseam'. He thinned out some of the chords, as the pianist's hands were very small. The piano writing for his songs is usually quite easy and effective—he does not, as has been claimed, write awkwardly for the instrument—but he sometimes does odd things. For example he writes like an organist on occasion. In the early song 'Through the Long Days' of 1885 some notes are irritatingly tied over from one chord to the next. This was the way in which professional organists were taught to play hymns and it is unsuitable for the piano. But this habit gradually disappears; Elgar's own piano arrangement of 'Dorabella', with Jaeger's help, is a brilliant transformation of an unyielding orchestral thought. In one case his use of the pedal is strangely insensitive over nearly two bars of introduction to the second verse of 'The Pipes of Pan.' However, when his songs have orchestral accompaniments, as this one does, we are in a world of tonecolour of a very different order. The five songs in the cycle known as *Sea Pictures* are not in fact all consistently good, but the ebb and flow of the sea and wind is so beautifully portrayed that we are deceived. Note the tranquil heaving of the swell in the first song, 'Sea SlumberSong', at the words 'I, the Mother mild' (letter B), with the strings three octaves deep and a sponge stick on the gong. This theme (which foreshadows Vaughan Williams), and the lovely opening bars, suggesting sleeping seabirds, are used again in the third song. His wife's own words provide an utterly simple second song in this cycle, which completes Elgar's 'first period'. Here and there the words are ineffectively, indeed incorrectly, set.[1]

Although encumbered frequently by the different conventions of his environment both in songs—popular ballads and patriotic airs—and in part-song—insipid sentiments—Elgar unexpectedly rises to the challenge of writing for unaccompanied chorus, with several telling results. Unexpected it seems, because he manages the solo voice so much more naturally than the chorus in his oratorios. He rarely strains the voices in their upward reaches, though he frequently takes the second basses too low for effective balance, e.g. the final chord, *fortissimo*, of 'O Wild West Wind', where, after a fine progression of harmonies, the whole structure rests on a bottom E flat. A similar ending comes to 'Love's Tempest', where the thinking is strong and passionate but somehow instrumental. Of the earlier part-songs, 'The Snow', with the happy idea of piano and two violins to go with the voices, is one of the best, while the five part-songs for unaccompanied male voices, from the Greek Anthology, contain some good ideas, especially the popular 'After many a dusty mile'. The eight-part chorus setting of Tennyson, 'There is Sweet Music' (Rome, December 1907), is in two keys at once. The female voices are written consistently in the key of A flat while the male voices are in G major. There is a good deal of ingenious alternation (including the final bars) and some modification, which produce a comparatively harmonious result, but pitching is difficult. Holst faced the same challenge with his six bitonal 'Canons' twenty-five years later. One of Elgar's joyous inspirations from Italy is 'Angelus' (Careggi, April 1909), where the imitation of bells and the cross rhythms arise easily from the voice parts.

[1] See Newman, *op. cit.*, pp. 121–6.

CHAPTER XII

THE SYMPHONIES

SOME wines, often the best, do not 'travel'. They used to need to be 'fortified' for the journey. It also often happens that only music which has been artificially 'spiced up' makes its mark in foreign countries. Certainly Elgar made few concessions to any alien tastes in spite of his predominantly 'continental' language. Hence the curious concept of his 'Englishness' which has apparently applied to his aloofness. One of the most persuasive advocates of the 'English' Elgar has been David Cox of the B.B.C., who gives three main headings: imperialist pageantry, the choral tradition and a 'particular kind of restraint'.[1] He continues by quoting the 'most passionate music', Gerontius's declaration of faith, 'Sanctus fortis', and then refers to Elgar's scoring with its meticulous detail. Taking the last point first, I must say that the almost fussy over-marking of parts which is such a feature of Elgar's orchestration cannot possibly be 'English'. Regarding the three main features, the only one which I would have accepted is the 'restraint', and only then if I believed that Elgar had it in the true 'English' sense—that is, as understatement—but Elgar usually wore his heart on his sleeve in a very un-English way, it seems to me. Assuredly, like some fine vintages, his music has never until very recently 'travelled' well; certainly not to the countries, Italy and America, which the composer so frequently visited. Like Mahler, this melancholy individual never came to terms with the particular way of life in which he grew up. But if, superficially, we can identify Mahler with the Austrian Empire it is because we recognize the sounds of the brilliant Vienna of an earlier epoch, whereas if Elgar's two symphonies fit into the splendid pageantry

[1] In *The Symphony*, vol. ii, ed. Robert Simpson (1967).

of the Edwardian era, there is yet nothing English about the actual sounds they make: no echo even of Elizabethan or folk music. What there is comes from abroad. The first magnificent sound, the motto theme of Symphony No. 1 in A flat (1908), has a phrase which almost certainly comes from Wagner:

Ex.8

(a) Wagner, *Parsifal*. End of first phrase *(Liebesmahl)*

(b) Elgar, *Symphony No.1*. Motto theme, penultimate phrase

In theory, therefore, this fine first symphony should have become a favourite work in Germany at least, but it has not done so. For this rejection I still cannot happily accept any 'Englishness' unless it be the subtle 'non-academic' approach, which so often was Elgar's starting point. In this instance it was the text-book rule that A flat major and D minor could not possibly be combined. Thus the introduction in the former key, *Andante, Nobilmente e semplice*, gives way to the first subject group, *Allegro*, in the latter; and the movement, looking as if it is to finish in A minor, strangely and beautifully settles down in A flat. Moreover the composer starts the Finale in D minor and later re-introduces his first idea in a splendid setting as a motto. The last bars of the symphony, marked *Grandioso*, give the final glitter. Another motive which is common to the first and last movements is made up of notes (see fig. 29) and seems like an incomplete note-row. It is so odd that one suspects that it is made out of the letters of someone's name:

Ex.9

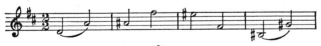

The two inner movements are linked since the fast pelting notes of the scherzo, *Allegro molto*, become the serene opening sequence of one of Elgar's sublimest slow movements. One of the com-poser's most unmistakable rising sequences (fig. 96) is followed by some of his loveliest chromatic harmony (two bars before fig. 98) and chains of arabesques. This is much stronger than a similar passage near the beginning of Charles Griffes's *The White Peacock*, 1915,[1] and more positive than the soft-edged floating driftwood of Delius, whose chromatically surging *Sea Drift* was first published in 1906. A profound movement is brought to an unforgettable close with alternating phrases on muted strings and muted trom-bones. The orchestration throughout the work has been virtuosic —note, for example, the rising chromatic scale on all four horns while the three trumpets hold a high G flat *crescendo molto* and *vibrato*, after fig. 46. This would have been a great symphony even if the second had not followed it three years later. Only one year after its production Lady Elgar wrote from Careggi, near Florence, to Lady Stuart of Wortley: 'My dearest Namesake. I have been wanting to send you a few lines from this lovely place and to tell you Edward is looking well and rested. I trust you will hear E's impressions, tonally, some day.' The new symphony, it seems, was on the way, as well as some part-songs.

There is something hectic about Symphony No. 2. Small figures treated sequentially dominate much of the intense writing of the first movement, *Allegro vivace e nobilmente*, and even the slow movement seems restlessly tragic rather than at peace. A constant battering at the ears of the listener pervades the third and apparently scherzo movement. The opening theme of the finale, *Moderato e maestoso*, originally designed to suit the tuba, suggests calm, but later drooping sequences soon tinge the movement with sadness. On the first page, in ink, Elgar wrote, 'Rarely, rarely, comest thou, Spirit of Delight!', but in pencil he drew another of his odd devils alongside. The autograph, on twenty-six-line manuscript paper, includes the writing-in of smudgy passages in blank spaces in red, and sometimes patches are stuck on. Lady Elgar, as usual, would

---

[1] Griffes returned to the United States from Berlin in 1907.

prepare the pages for full orchestra, but at fig. 33 he had to alter her lay-out for four pages so that there would be fewer staves for wood-wind, leaving room for divided strings. Even so the side-drum and bass drum get added below the bottom stave. The passage between fig. 46 and fig. 49 is not in his hand; it is copied from fig. 8 a tone down, and Elgar added the altered timpani figure.

How did Elgar compose? The slow movement of this sym-phony offers an interesting example. From the sketches, which were sent to Lady Stuart of Wortley in March 1911 and be-queathed by her to the Birthplace, we can see that a certain single 'clash' sound came first in his mind for this movement (originally marked *Adagio*). There were also some rejected ideas not sent to her but found after his death by his daughter and sent to Lady Stuart of Wortley's daughter. He writes of 'clashes', 'later' and 'together', but does not in fact do what he had in mind. Here is one of the relevant sketches, in which the first chord is the 'clash', which was finally used with such restraint:

Ex. 10

crossed out
and marked
'later'   etc.

The published version, in fact, contains the following poignant phrase at the beginning and ending of the movement only, and it will be seen that the 'clash' chord, marked with an asterisk, is now the seventh:

Ex. 11

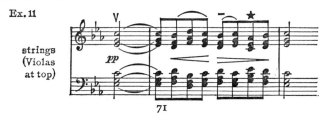

strings
(Violas
at top)

It is not even marked with any sort of *sforzando* and yet the sketches had constantly harped on it. It is as if the black despair, akin to Tchaikovsky's in his sixth symphony, has been purged and refined. The sketches also included the combination of this idea with the first subject proper (at fig. 67)—a brass theme which comes back later (at fig. 79) with some of the most impressive full orchestra decoration written by any composer, through which a plaintive oboe weaves its solitary, but clearly audible, way.

The scherzo movement, *Rondo: presto*, is mainly a fierce *moto perpetuo* with cross rhythms, but a lovely middle section tune, associated with Lady Stuart of Wortley, as 'Windflower' is written on the sketch, appeared first in this weaker form (a). The final version (b) has the stronger drop from F sharp to C.

Like the *Enigma*, the first subject of the last movement employs a severely restricted rhythmic pattern. Later it becomes, as Harriet Cohen put it, 'like a molten blaze of sunlight across a great sky'. 'One can't hear anything at all after it,' Lawrence of Arabia said to her, 'it kills all other music.' [1] Was it the string of sequences that grows out of the end of the second subject after fig. 140 that Miss Cohen and Walton were thinking of when they joked about Elgar's descending sequences? The composer wrote out the initial phrase, they decided, and then went out for a walk, leaving Lady Elgar to complete them, right down to the last one in the bass.[2] It

[1] Cohen, *op. cit.*, p. 149.
[2] *Ibid.*, p. 167.

was, of course, a joke. Sequences had flowed throughout Elgar's artistic career like life-blood. They only cheapened the stereotyped music which already had little value; they enriched those finer passages which were already pulsating with originality. Here they seem to have the tragic last word.

Just before the recapitulation (four bars before fig. 156), the composer wrote in the autograph over a static passage: 'Art made tongue-tied by authority.' The ending is like a sunset. Some would suggest that it represents the sunset of the British Empire. Elgar, at any rate, knew that values were changing and a way of life was going. Music to elevate, exalt and ennoble would no longer be required. A glance at Appendix A at the end of this book will show that the first writers of the 'new music' were already active at this time: Schönberg was thirty-seven, Bartók thirty, while Hindemith, Hába and Křenek were in their teens and Dallapiccola was seven. Music was soon to lose nationality; the question of 'Englishness' would fade away for ever, while music, like architecture, became not even international, but rather non-national. Even Wilfrid Mellers was sufficiently disturbed by listening to a performance of the Second Symphony after a weekend of experimental music to be astonished at what had happened in sixty years.[1] Is there a patronizing tone in 'Elgar's heroic, noble, prideful, tender, frenzied, melancholy (*etc.*) assertion of human will and consciousness' compared with the 'de-humanizing mutterings and mumblings' of the present day, and does his sociological approach solve this problem? Our culture, he claims, has been responsible also for the horrors behind Elgar's jingoism.

[1] *Musical Times*, October 1968, p. 922.

CHAPTER XIII

CONCERTOS

ELGAR destroyed a youthful violin concerto in 1890 and from 1909 to 1932 toyed on and off with the idea of a piano concerto. There remain then only two complete concertos in his output: the Concerto for Violin and Orchestra, Op. 61, of 1910 and the Concerto for Violoncello and Orchestra, Op. 85, of 1919. Basil Maine suggested that the symphonies 'make us aware of life primarily in terms of conflict and action; [but the Violin Concerto] carries us to the safe retreat of the contemplative life'.[1] Like other commentators, he seemed unaware of the intense inner conflict in Elgar which went into the Violin Concerto, which is as *unsafe* a retreat as any, although the musical language has become more refined. The move backwards to Schumann, the *fons et origo* which was to become so pronounced in the 'third' period, has already started. Schumann's influence is at its most powerful in the first movement—for example the groups of four chords repeated many times after fig. 12; and yet by the time the music has reached fig. 15, little more than a minute later, its angular leaps already anticipate Walton. The most telling part of the opening structure is that the orchestral *tutti* leads one to the point where one would expect the soloist's entry, but the soloist slips in unobtrusively two bars late and then blandly finishes the phrase on the tonic, as if the concerto had ended before it started. By a series of rhapsodic phrases, alternately faltering or urgent, the soloist lifts the work off the ground and it soars. By its opulent yet balanced scoring this work is like the symphonies, but by its constant changes of tempo (what Miss McVeagh calls 'minute quickenings and dallyings'[2]) it is

---

[1] *Op. cit.*, vol. ii, p. 140.
[2] *Op. cit.*, p. 167.

like the sort of piece that an Italian would have written for a sensitive *prima donna*.

No genuine old-fashioned *prima donna* would be very pleased in the slow movement, however, to discover that the main theme, in the mood of Brahms's Violin Concerto, is given to the orchestra; and the soloist, when he enters, is always given a counter-melody. The flowing music, suggesting perhaps Puccini and Tchaikovsky on the way, reaches a sublime moment six bars after fig. 53, where the violinist plays demi-semiquaver arabesques but the orchestra is significantly marked *nobilmente*. Elgar must have known instinc-tively that this was the 'best of him', since he quotes this phrase again in the finale (at fig. 94). The intensely personal middle part of the slow movement rises to an impassioned climax at fig. 56, after which the music falls away as if exhausted, the first horn repeating a falling sixth and the soloist playing slow *appoggiaturas* until the recapitulation—where, again, the soloist is still not per-mitted to play the theme.

Back again from B flat major to B minor, the last movement, *Allegro molto*, takes us into the world of the great virtuosos—the cascading chromatic chords between figs. 65 and 66, so up-to-date in 1910, were very much the stock-in-trade of Elgar's experiment-ing but less talented contemporaries. He understood the violin as no other great composer and he needed no Joachim to edit his music, although one is reminded of Brahms in the phrase which first appears one bar after fig. 72. The most unexpectedly magical feature of this movement is the *cadenza accompagnata* where the strings are told that the *pizzicato tremolando* should be 'thrummed' with the soft part of three or four fingers, while the soloist muses at length, recalling ideas from the first movement.

Nine years later Elgar has changed: perhaps now there is a retreat from the world, and this I have called the 'third' period. It includes the three chamber music pieces and also the Violoncello Concerto. Apart from the elasticity in the motto theme which appears at the beginnings of the first, second and fourth move-ments, there is less of that Elgarian eager hurrying and shy holding back; there is considerably less weight in the orchestra too, though it may be argued that this arises naturally from the problem of balance that every cello concerto presents. More striking still, the harmonic language has retreated strangely so that there is hardly a progression in the short third movement, *Adagio*, that Schumann would not have enjoyed. In fact, had it appeared nearly a century earlier, he might have reviewed it in his *Neue Zeitschrift* and said, 'Hats off, gentlemen. A genius.' Even so, there is a newness here every bit as personal as the more obvious later French influence in the fleet and fleeting *scherzo*, the second movement. Tucked away in this movement, indeed, is one of Elgar's stray thoughts that no one else could have written—a sort of tiny second subject.

The mood of the whole work is subdued and resigned; and although the Finale, *Allegro non troppo*, looks like being a hearty reminder of happier days, this movement gives way to a melancholy as deep as anything the composer has yet expressed (at fig. 66). The drooping sequences which follow (at fig. 69) manage to avoid the commonplace in much the same way that Verdi's beautiful motive in *Otello* does—by the chromatic raising of the expected last note by a semitone. The note is marked with an asterisk in each case:

Ex.13
(a) Verdi, *Otello*, End of Act I

(b) Elgar

Although the two concertos dovetail with the two symphonies in time, that for cello is a work apart, by a lonely man in war-time who sees that artistic criteria have altered irreversibly.

When the soloist is for the second time exulting in the swaggering tune of the finale at fig. 59, it may come as a shock to him to discover that a dozen or so cellists of a full symphony orchestra are playing with him at the unison. Except while playing in the *tuttis* of a Baroque concerto, soloists do not expect this: it is typical of Elgar's 'not leave well alone' scoring. The idea of constantly touching up, smoothing over, blending and blurring colours and strengthening tone is much like the contemporary brass-band scoring: Elgar naturally took to the scoring of his *Severn Suite* with an easier grace than many of the other 'serious' composers who ventured into that unfamiliar field at the time and later. We may also think back to the cadenza of the Violin Con-certo. Again he will 'not leave well alone' and the soloist has attendants, though producing a lovely mysterious discreet thrum-ming which is like a Spanish serenade, especially the guitarist's chords six bars after fig. 103.

A word or two on the Spanish influence on Elgar may now be appropriate. He never visited Spain and yet time and time again a Spanish flavour affects his music. Many of his early trifles, from *Sevillaña*, reveal it in the harmony and rhythm, while semi-Moorish melodic inflexions are to be found in the 'Sérénade Mauresque' as well as in the weird dance in *The Black Knight*. But what of the rhythm for the ill Gerontius (at fig. 4), what of the swaying chords in the *Introduction and Allegro* (at fig. 10)? These chords move, by the way, to a syncopated rhythm which Elgar seems unconsciously to have repeated in the solo line of the second movement of the Cello Concerto (cf. *Introduction and Allegro*, fig. 10, and the concerto, one bar after fig. 20). Gervase Hughes[1] thinks that the Gerontius motive may owe something to Sullivan's *The Rose of Persia* (1899). Also Elgar had contemplated setting Belloc's 'Spanish' poem 'Tarantella' (later set by Francis Toye). Then there is the strange influence of the legend of the impious Spanish monks at Flexham Park, which must have affected both harmony and rhythm of the second subject of the Piano Quintet.[2]

---

[1] *The Music of Arthur Sullivan* (1960), p. 72.
[2] The story is apparently a modern myth. For a detailed discussion see the foreword by Michael Pope to the Eulenberg miniature score of the Piano Quintet (London, 1971).

Finally the composer tried to complete an opera which had been on his mind for a very long period, *The Spanish Lady*. It seems as if he had been drawn as by the memory of a previous existence. An interesting radio programme, using the 180 fragments, edited by Percy Young, was broadcast by B.B.C. 4, Midland, on 15th December 1969. Dr Young had fully scored many of the items, some of which made quite a strong impression: only one page, of four bars, had been written in full score by the composer. Of course a fugue was used for the 'diabolical behaviour' of Meercraft, a plausible rogue. The final 'Bolero' is exciting, if more like a polonaise than anything Spanish. The opera was gradually dropped by the end of 1932, and it is very difficult to decide whether the work would have held the stage as the composer had earlier wished.[1]

[1] A whole chapter is devoted to the work in Percy Young's *Elgar O.M.*

CHAPTER XIV

CHAMBER MUSIC AND KEYBOARD MUSIC

THE main paradox of Elgar's three mature chamber music works is that in one sense the composer has too few instruments yet in another he has too many. His thought, like Haydn's, was often in two or three parts: a melody, a bass and sometimes a counter-melody—and this may account for his sometimes doubling alto and tenor lines. But much of his orchestral writing 'blows up' the texture so that, most important, he cannot refrain from demanding a large number of instruments to colour, to thicken, to underline, to highlight and, in innumerable ways, to touch up all three basic lines. Thus writing for a string quartet alone was an unusual experience and a challenge for him.

Another curious feature is his apparently unadventurous style in 1918. It appears that he left his sketches in London when he went down to Brinkwells.[1] This may be the reason why the style has become so refined, though the war obviously affected him also. Gone are the brash, brassy modernisms. He is content instead to play about with formal differences in a more conservative idiom, being avowedly out of touch with new music. There are mannerisms, of some of which he was fond, which to later ears are rather tiresome. The progression deriving from Wagner in the Piano Quintet is referred to below in the chapter on harmonic language. The melancholy doodling on a dominant minor ninth or a dreary series of diminished sevenths in the same work, in the second movement at fig. 32, shows Brahms all too clearly as its inspiration. The stronger series of *arpeggios* in the Violin Sonata at fig. 5, thought by Reed to come from listening to the wind rustling an Aeolian harp,[2] has a more Slavonic origin. The constant pedal

[1] Young, *op. cit.*, p. 345.
[2] *Elgar as I knew him*, p. 149.

idea (low G) with changing harmonies runs through all the Russians from Balakirev to Tchaikovsky.

It seems that, instead of breaking away from the procedures of the past, Elgar now prefers to take sonata form with its system of keys and gently to break its rules—with a quiet chuckle to himself as he does so. Seventeen years before this he had chuckled that his first *Pomp and Circumstance* march, although in D major, had started on E flat. Now, for those who are sympathetic to him, there are some beautiful but gentle surprises. Not only does the Violin Sonata start in the 'wrong' key—A minor instead of E minor—but it maintains the deception right up to the penultimate bar of the movement. The second movement alternates a fancy, which is like a grave dance from an unwritten ballet, with a strongly lyrical second subject. This first idea is in Elgar's best *salon* manner. The finale, more solemn, is somewhat disappointing, but it does quote the lovely second subject of the second movement: Elgar here, as in the Violin Concerto, had a knack of knowing what was the best of him.

Simultaneously the other two compositions were being worked on and the creative flame was burning high. The idea which had delighted him before in the exposition of the Violin Concerto is now exploited in the Piano Quintet: that of coming to a full stop in the home key at the ends of opening phrases. He boldly plays this dangerous game at the sixth bar and again at the seventeenth. Moreover, when the introduction is over, the following *Allegro* also crashes to a halt almost before it has got under way. One cannot help believing that Elgar actually wanted to see the old fogies of the Germanic school wagging their heads ruefully at his misdeeds. This work uses the Franckian idea of a motto theme returning in the finale in a somewhat conventional way, but it also uses diverse ideas in juxtaposition, rather as the great oratorios had done. A peculiar 'Spanish' idea in the first movement (after fig. 4) gives way to a jaunty tune (fig. 6) before returning to the original idea (in the *Allegro* there is a metamorphosis of the introductory bars). There is some ordinary 'working out' which does not add much, and ordinary bass notes become busy, as they have done so many times before: for example, in *Pomp and Circumstance*, March No. 1, two bars before E, and even in his edition of 'God Save the King'—a phrase from the first bar of *Froissart*. But he does also sometimes use the newer technique of short repeated units which do not develop in the old classical way. Typical of this are the one-bar motives at fig. 25 in the slow movement of the String Quartet. There are less obvious sequences—but what is Elgar without this essentially classical device? It is clear here that with the four string players Elgar welcomes the idea of returning to the world of classical Vienna: the interplay of intimate voices as in Beethoven. Just as cadences in late Beethoven become increasingly back-to-front and strangely consonant, so do Elgar's, e.g. this from the Quartet:

Ex.14

The String Quartet's last movement, starting as if from Eastcheap with Falstaff, ends in a gay rhythmic cavalcade in which it seems that hordes of 'Little Bells', 'Bears' and 'Bavarians' invade the score. In the last bar but two in the manuscript Elgar has crossed out the upper octaves for the first violin. It is as if he had told himself that a good quartet must not have a concerto part for the leader—again part of the paradox.

What of Elgar's supposed awkwardness when writing for the keyboard? It is certainly there in the Piano Quintet, and Young makes a good point when, concerning the Sonata, he thinks he might have learnt from Brahms—and 'Brahms might very well have been glad to have written so miraculously for violin'.[1] Be this

---

[1] *Op. cit.*, p. 349.

as it may, Elgar had had considerable experience. He successfully made his own piano arrangements of the orchestral part in many choral works and of such essentially instrumental textures as the Violin Concerto. 'I have no opinion,' he said to Basil Maine,[1] 'of the composer who can only think in terms of the keyboard.' There is nothing awkward in the many early piano accompaniments, while most of the solos for piano from *May Song* (1901), with its Schubertian changes of key, to the delightfully easy *Sonatina* (1932) for May Grafton, his niece, are completely professional. As one would expect, there is not the brilliance that one finds in the unaccompanied violin *Études Caractéristiques* (published in 1892), but the composer can manage the keyboard and he can manage manuals and pedals too. The Organ Sonata, Op. 28 of 1895, is superior to the Eleven Vesper Voluntaries of 1889 not in competence but in personality. In fact the sonata is one of the first early works of Elgar which has the character of the great composer stamped all over it, and which must still be assessed in his total output.

On 9th January 1969, *The Times* announced that John Ogdon would give the first public performance for sixty years of the 'lost' Concert Allegro at the Cardiff Festival on March 2nd. Although influenza in fact prevented Ogdon from playing on this occasion he had edited and in February broadcast the work, which had been written for Fanny Davies in 1901. The manuscript was discovered by Mrs Bernard in August 1968 in the library of her late husband, the conductor Anthony Bernard. But although a certain excitement has attached to the discovery after over sixty years and though Ogdon declares the work is well written for the medium, there is very little in it that proclaims the master hand.

[1] *Op. cit.*, vol. i, p. 212.

CHAPTER XV

ELGAR'S HARMONIC LANGUAGE

ALTHOUGH Elgar naturally fell in with the Germanic chromati-
cized major-minor system of the late nineteenth century, it is true
to say that some of his most characteristic utterances were in
conflict with these influences. Much of his music is non-Germanic;
much of his very finest music is diatonic; and frequently he
uses an impure form of the minor key—Percy Young thinks the
'whimsical treatment of minor tonality' comes from Mendelssohn.[1]
To take the last point first, it would not be true to say of his minor
writing that it is modal, any more than it would be true of that of
Dvořák or Grieg; but from a sketch of 1878,[2] through the opening
bars of *King Olaf* (the saga motive), through the song published in
1900, 'The Pipes of Pan', the *Grania and Diarmid* funeral march,
'The Tame Bear' in the second *Wand of Youth* Suite, etc., to the
first interlude in *Falstaff*, Page to the Duke (see Ex. 23 below), the
'Nineveh' section of *The Music Makers* (fig. 28), the *Serenade* Op.
73, No. 2 for unaccompanied voices, and the opening of the
Piano Quintet, etc., there is a strangely personal use of the flat
seventh. It is neither the correct 'descending form of the scale' of
the text-book nor the more 'folky' modal treatment which was
later to be exploited by Vaughan Williams and his followers. The
opening motive of *King Olaf* is described by Newman—rightly—
as 'extremely effective',[3] but nowadays we can look back at some
of Elgar's most admired passages and see them as somewhat

[1] *Op. cit.*, p. 277.
[2] *Ibid.*, p. 383.
[3] Newman, *op. cit.*, p. 18.

derivative. Did Newman in 1904 not see that the end of the Introduction (used again at the end of the Cantata) is much more individual than the beginning?

And what of the very first bass note in the Violin Concerto? Is this not almost perversely flat, almost like a misprint to the uninitiated? Bars 3 and 4 of *Pomp and Circumstance*, No. 2, go through the same motions.

Elgar frequently alternated the minor key with the tonic major rather than the relative major. The only classical composer to make a serious feature of this was Schubert. Elgar also preferred the minor tonality—and it might even be said that in particular he liked G minor: the key of one of his earliest pieces, a Fugue for organ of about 1870 (see Chapter VII). 'Fugue was a form which often curiously and fantastically fired his imagination,' said Percy Young [1]—but Elgar was always unorthodox.

The self-taught Elgar has often been contrasted with the 'academic' Englishman, Irishman and Scotsman: Parry, Stanford and Mackenzie. Sometimes, however, he is indistinguishable.[2]

---

[1] *Op. cit.*, p. 269.

[2] See 'Allusiveness in Musical Composition', a lecture delivered at Cardiff by H. A. Harding, Mus.D., F.R.C.O., 13th April 1909. Printed for the R.C.O., 1910.

Ex.16

(a) Mackenzie. *The Dream of Jubal* (Funeral March) 1889

Molto maestoso

(b) Elgar *Sea Pictures* (No.5 The Swimmer) July 1899

Allegro di molto

Elgar conducted the Mackenzie work in Worcester on 4th May 1899.

And what are those formerly admired chromatic passages but new toys that had already been played with? Wagner, who changed the face of the musical map, included in his innovations the 'weak' resolution of chords, as seen in the 'Liebestod' from *Tristan* and the 'Reine Thor-motive' in *Parsifal*, but one of these devices occurs as early as *Tannhäuser*, completed in 1845 and an opera which Elgar knew as early as 1883, when he arranged a part of it for piano.

This not only got into *King Olaf*, the arresting wailing of the wind and dashing of the foam (vocal score p. 21) which comes again at Olaf's death (p. 153), but it gets into *Gerontius* in many new forms. The first striking example of this sliding harmony here is at 'Go, in the name of Angels and Archangels' (fig. 72) and a later one is when Gerontius goes before his Judge (after fig. 115):

Ex.17

(a) Wagner

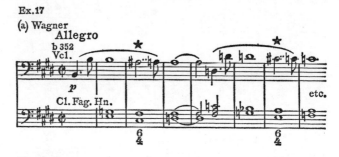

(b) Elgar

Although it is the 'leading note' (starred in both examples) which limply falls instead of rising in both Wagner and Elgar, it can be seen that the latter is now writing something different and distinctly personal.

The middle part of the 'Agnus Dei' of Fauré's *Requiem* (1887) is also Wagnerian but yet different. For the technically minded some of it can be put thus: whereas Wagner uses an irregular second inversion (marked ⁶₄), Elgar introduces a 'weak' suspension on a first inversion (marked ⁶₄–3), which is new. Elgar loathed the rules of the theorists. Is it coincidence that they always call the 7–6 and the ⁵₄–3 (but not this ⁶₄) 'strong'? These Wagnerian harmonies in different guises became a mannerism: e.g. 'Owls' (bar 5) and the

Piano Quintet, first movement at fig. 1. The theory of suspensions comes ultimately from the practice of the sixteenth century; and Elgar, like Beethoven, used in his own way only such ideas from antiquity as he liked. When he writes the more usual suspensions or *appoggiaturas*, he usually involves the 'forbidden' tritone. Climaxes of phrases frequently use this almost as a fingerprint, as in some of the loudest parts of the orchestral *tutti* of the Violin Concerto (between figs. 3 and 4), for example; but surely never in a more evocatively lovely way than with the softest insistence in the slow movement (between figs. 56 and 57) before the recapitulation. In so far as the former climactic chord, with high-lying strings and punching trombone entry, is virtually identical with a similar moment (three bars before fig. 4) in the first of the *Enigma Variations*, 'C.A.E.', one might even suppose that the 'soul' of the Violin Concerto was, after all, that of the composer's beloved wife. The 'Et incarnatus' from Beethoven's *Missa Solemnis* suggests that the composer studied the older counterpoint and then forgot it, just as the 'Apostles' motive—see the Prelude to *The King-dom*, bars 7 to 9—is a *nota cambiata* only in general shape, not in treatment.

For the non-Germanic—let alone non-English—sound in Elgar's language, we may take a further look at the Violin Concerto. The opening theme, with its optimistic outburst soon to be tinged with melancholy, is not typical of Tchaikovsky, but the reappearance of this theme on the horns in the major key during the work's final seven bars most surely is. In fact it is just the sort of thing that the Russian composer does with one of the principal themes, also in B minor, in *Swan Lake*. The mixed-colour scoring (fig. 10), furthermore, in the first movement of the Violin Concerto is thoroughly un-German. It again recalls *Swan Lake*: the famous waltz in Act I. It is, of course, un-English, because there was no such thing as English scoring (notice the different nuances: solo violin *ff*; three horns *pp*; and basses *p*), and the only composer who had recently written anything at all like this work in harmonic language was MacDowell, in the last movement of his *Sonata Tragica* for piano (1893).

But, much though Elgar seems to have shared Tchaikovsky's melancholy, so also was he able to share the spirit of the lighter and more cheerful *salon* pieces. The dancing of 'Dorabella' and the brass of 'E.D.U.' (himself) also owe something to the Russian. If he had been a Russian, said Elgar much later on, the *Enigma Variations* would have been a ballet. And in 1968 they were finally made into one by Frederick Ashton. If Ravel thought that Elgar's language was 'in effect Mendelssohn',[1] then Ravel must have been thinking of the very earliest *salon* pieces (did he know the *Romance*, Op. 1, 1878?); if not, he was indeed very insensitive to stylistic detail or perhaps just deliberately ignorant.

Of course Elgar does not slavishly follow Tchaikovsky. For instance, when he has just had the instruments the right way round, you will find an inversion of violin parts such as this from the *Introduction and Allegro*:

Ex. 18
bar after ⑤

Tempo primo

Strings

Reminding one possibly of the nervous twisting of string lines in the final movement of Tchaikovsky's *Pathetic Symphony*, this nevertheless represents the practical Elgar: he gives the second fiddles the limelight. In the Symphony No. 1 he goes even further: he gives the last desks of all the strings the tune (in the last movement at fig. 146). This is tremendously practical and original. It is also diatonic, like the quotation above, which has cascading

[1] In Vaughan Williams's 'Musical Autobiography', quoted fully in H. Foss, *Ralph Vaughan Williams* (1950), p. 35.

clashes more in the tradition of Bach (the organ *Toccata* in F major, for example) than that of the Romantics:

Ex. 19

(a) Bach, *Toccata* in F, BWV. 540

(b) Elgar, *Pomp & Circumstance* March No. 1, bar 15.

(c) Elgar, *Gerontius* Part II (before ③):

But the later Romantics had been exploiting new progressions. Another 'new look' had been coming in: a major sub-dominant chord, often with seventh or ninth added (Elgar plays with it in fig. 5 of the *Light of Life*, 1896)—*see* Examples 20*a* and 20*b* below.

Ex. 20

(a) Sullivan, *The Golden Legend*, Sc. VI (1886)

(b) Puccini, *Manon Lescaut*,
Act III (1893)

In his ding-dong use of two chords, Elgar follows Sullivan, is paralleled by Puccini and Fauré and anticipates the Vaughan Williams of *On Wenlock Edge* (third song, 1911). These chords, somewhat extended, are exploited at the end of Fauré's song 'Clair de Lune' (1887), for example. Elgar makes use of these sounds as small units and he also likes to move them up and down:

Ex. 21
Elgar, *The Kingdom*, Sc. IV (1906)

repeated and
transposed

Similar four-chord units, deriving ultimately from Wagner, form a rather tiresome feature of *Falstaff* (figs. 19–21). Elgar was sufficiently 'taken' by his own sequences here to ink in the sketches (? August 1913). The extraordinary thing is that these seemingly 'modern' effects are now forgotten. The most lasting Elgar—and therefore the most true Elgar—is not to be found here, nor in the Debussyan consecutive fifths of *Gerontius* (fig. 108), and still less in the even lusher slide-slipping of the later oratorios, culminating with the ninths and thirteenths of *The Music Makers* (fig. 43). These sounds have become dated. As one might expect, it is the 'still small voice' of unpretentiousness which has given Elgar the stamp of genius. And the two-chord units which are now remembered are either wholly diatonic (*The Wand of Youth* and the Organ Sonata) or nearly so, with the supertonic imaginary root being used (*Chanson de Matin*):

Ex.22
(a) *The Wand of Youth*
(from 1879)

(b) *Organ Sonata* (1895),
second movt.

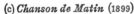

(c) *Chanson de Matin* (1899)

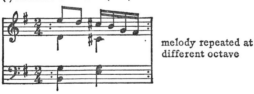

melody repeated at
different octave

Sometimes the two-chord unit is expanded sequentially, as in *Caractacus* (1898), sc. 3 (at fig. 1).

Just as the Russian Nationalists had the problem of fitting their tunes into the obsessively uniform bed of German harmony, which never comfortably accepted their falling fourths, so Elgar's melodic line never really lent itself either to the main stream. Typical of this is what Elgar himself called the 'cheerful, out-of-doors, ambling theme' in *Falstaff*. His treatment is naturally in two parts—and he does not really care about orthodox treatment—and then he adds a holding note (figs. 36 and 53 for example). A student of Tovey's suggested that, although for full orchestra, *Falstaff* consisted entirely of two-part harmony.[1] This may be exaggerated, but much of Elgar's thinking is initially of two lines: a melody and a bass.

[1] *Op cit.*, vol. iv.

CHAPTER XVI

ELGAR'S STRUCTURE, COLOUR AND INFLUENCE

IF ELGAR has been criticized for the detail of his writing, the chromaticism and the sequences, etc., he has been criticized even more for his structures. What he enjoyed was in the music. At his zenith he was as prodigal with his material as Sullivan had been. He would certainly have echoed Sullivan's advice to Dame Ethel Smyth: 'We composers have to make a shillingsworth of music for a penny—and here you go throwing away guineas.' But, like the Sullivan of *The Mikado*, Elgar was brimming with ideas: putting them together was a skilled occupation but a secondary matter to the urgent business of creating. Elgar would also have agreed with Sibelius: 'Preserve the themes of your youth; they are the best you will ever invent.' He was not content with the con-cocted abstractions of dullards but, when needing ideas for a new work, he constantly turned and re-turned the pages of his old sketch-books. Extremely well-read in the literary classics, he was also an enthusiast for the great classical composers. It is not sur-prising, therefore, that his music should so often be unashamedly full of sequences. Percy Young may be right to say that the use of sequence as early as 1871 is 'straight from the text-book',[1] but Elgar would never have retained such a device if he had not found it also in living music. What 'came off' in Bach also suited Elgar, and it was frequently a structural device for propelling the music forward. Even so, using ideas from his sketch-books, he also employed the method of integrating small original units into his music. I have already described this as a more modern device and, looking back now, we can see the older, conservative classical building process being frequently thrust aside. Newman did not

[1] *Op. cit.*, p. 271.

understand this when he thought some of *The Apostles* was built as if by children 'putting together painted blocks of wood'.[1]

These 'units' were nearly always instrumental rather than vocal. When they are used in the big choral works, it is easy to see how notes are twisted or repeated to suit voices. Even with such significant lines as 'They shall grow not old, as we that are left grow old' ('For the Fallen', fig. 19), the voice parts are an obvious addition to the texture. Only the solo voice, with 'we will remember them', has its natural line and its characteristic Italianate pause, which halts the orchestra. Elgar is kind to his soloists. To some extent, he started where Wagner finished: the main thought was usually in the orchestra.[2] He was, however, a portrait painter (dedicating most of his works to sympathetic people, despite his favouring of 'absolute' music in his Birmingham lectures). The *Variations* are a gallery of friends, the oratorios are about New Testament characters, the Violin Concerto enshrines someone's soul, and the *Sea Pictures* are not empty seascapes. The ultimate achievement in this respect is his 'study' of *Falstaff*, where he sees no need for singers; almost certainly he is happier without their personification. Richard Strauss, on the other hand, did the opposite; he left his earlier symphonic poems and turned to opera during the course of his prolific career. Modern though he sounded then, Strauss is now seen as less original and lasting than Elgar. We may be thankful that Ken Russell, who produced such a fanatically hostile fantasy-portrait of Strauss, *The Dance of the Seven Veils*, on B.B.C. Television on 15th February 1970, gave us a comparatively down-to-earth, sane and friendly picture of Elgar in his film first shown on B.B.C. Television on 11th November 1962.

Falstaff is a curious work also in that the two Interludes actually sound like reminiscences from an earlier world. And yet, with their 'static' and non-symphonic quality, they are remarkably modern; the only older composer who comes to mind is the untaught, crude but vivid Mussorgsky—Elgar must often have wanted to escape from the main stream by parading his lack of formal training. The

[1] *Op cit.*, p. 102.
[2] See Reed, *op. cit.*, p. 150.

94

first, the 'Dream Interlude' at fig. 76, consists almost entirely of one tune, a most characteristic one, repeated over and over again. All the composer does to it, as with many others, including the *Enigma* theme (first six bars) and the opening of Symphony No. I at its first repeat appearance, is to add a scrap of counterpoint (in *Dream Children*, No. 2, it is the middle section tune which gets this treatment):

Ex. 23   **Poco Allegretto**

I know few people who do not find themselves constantly humming this tune—not the countersubject, although no Elgarian can fail to note the stamp of personality here—when it has recently been played. The sheer repetitiveness has an almost hypnotic effect, more akin to Eastern music than the European tradition. The second episode, likewise, is just an alternation of ideas. Perhaps, with Hans Keller, we may talk of 'conservative progressiveness' [1] here.

Another really progressive quality which cannot be overlooked is Elgar's masterly concern with colour. If the second subject of the 'Romance' movement of the mature Sonata for Violin and Piano, Op. 82, sounds superficially like something from the Germanic past, the one feature which marks it out as belonging to Elgar's world (and the later twentieth century) is the composer's continual preoccupation with heard sound as opposed to academic development. Whether the violin soars (fig. 32) or dips down to the G string (four bars before fig. 31), the composer is utterly absorbed in the sonorities of the instrument. It goes without saying that Elgar will contrive that a recapitulation in the Violin Concerto will give him the same opportunity for double-stopping with an open string (cf. two bars before fig. 22 with two bars before fig. 41)—although he writes significantly on the sketch: 'These passages must lead "on".' Very few composers, if any, have been more fastidious in indicating their exact intentions with such loving care. As early as 1898 Elgar knew his own orchestration was good, and he described Parry's as 'dead and never more than an *organ part arranged*'.[1] Once Elgar's was written he never changed a thing. Meyerbeer's plan of writing alternative scorings in different coloured inks to find out how they sounded was a favourite subject of derision with him.[2]

Elgar's influence has not at first been apparent. Some minor composers have absorbed something from him; the biggest followers have been Vaughan Williams, Bliss and Walton. Vaughan Williams said modestly: 'I am astonished . . . how much I cribbed from him, probably when I thought I was being most original.'[3] Which of these extracts would strike one as Elgar and which Walton?

Ex. 24

[1] Letter to Jaeger, 9th March 1898.
[2] Reed, *Elgar as I knew him*, p. 149.
[3] *Music and Letters*, xvi, No. 1.

The first, from *Gerontius* (two bars before fig. 106), contains what was known as a 'certain appalling chord' (letter to D. Ffrangcon-Davies, 30th December 1902) [1]—though the progression had actually occurred in *Caractacus*, sc. 3, after fig. 12. The second extract is from *Belshazzar's Feast* (at fig. 11) which appeared thirty-one years later. Gerald Finzi is one of the minor composers who gets as near as anyone to the true nobility of an Elgar slow movement in his own Cello Concerto. William Wordsworth's sad-voiced Symphony No. 1 of 1944, with its ambiguous tonal centres and angular leaps, uses to some extent a post-*Falstaff* idiom. Finally, 'light music' would never have been what it is without the *Pomp and Circumstance* marches—for example Eric Coates's popular *Knightsbridge* march from the *London Suite* of 1933.

What was Elgar's greatest achievement? One school of thought, including the composer's leading biographers, says it was *Gerontius*, which, they claim, has unity. For the composer, at the time, 'this is the best of me . . . this, if anything of mine, is worth your memory'. I can find no more unity in the small sections which are fitted together here than in Elgar's other great works; and the poem is no more unified than the many inferior verses also set by him, though it does certainly have classical continuity. Another school of thought, preferring a more secular and less tragic subject, chooses *Falstaff*. Again the composer is with them and frequently said he thought it the 'highest point he had reached in the production of a purely orchestral work'.[2] Again I beg to suggest that the composer may not be the best judge. A third school, a minority,

[1] Marjorie Ffrangcon-Davies, *David Ffrangcon-Davies* (1938), pp. 33-4.
[2] Reed, *op. cit.*, p. 113.

makes a plea for the chamber music, but this cannot in all seriousness be supported. I will end by making what may seem a more extravagant claim: not only did Elgar accept Jaeger's challenge, but he actually wrote four or five superb slow movements which really do measure up to the greatest in Beethoven. These, the greatest of him in spite of his own modesty about them, are surely:

1899   'Nimrod'
1908   The slow movement of Symphony No. 1
1910   The slow movement of the Violin Concerto
1911   The slow movement of Symphony No. 2

To which we might add:

1906   'The Sun goeth down' (from *The Kingdom*)

These movements contain his most mature and personal musical thoughts—and they can move to tears.

APPENDICES

APPENDIX A

CALENDAR

(Figures in brackets denote the age reached by the person mentioned during the year in question.)

Year	Age	Life	Contemporary Musicians
1857		Edward William Elgar born Broadheath, June 2, son of W. H. Elgar, tuner, organist and later music dealer in Worcester (business established 1841). Siblings: Harry aged 7, Lucy aged 4, Pollie aged 2.	Glinka (54) dies, Feb. 15; Auber 75; Balakirev 20; Balfe 49; Sterndale Bennett 41; Berlioz 54; Berwald 61; Bizet 19; Boito 15; Borodin 24; Brahms 24; Bruch 19; Bruckner 33; Chabrier 16; Chausson 2; Cowen 5; Cui 22; Dargomizhsky 44; Delibes 21; Duparc 9; Dvořák 16; Fauré 12; Franck 35; Gade 40; Gounod 39; Grieg 14; Halévy 58; Humperdinck 3; d'Indy 6; Janáček 3; Lalo 34; Liadov 2; Liszt 46; Mackenzie 10; Marschner 62; Meyerbeer 66; Mussorgsky 18; Offenbach 38; Hubert Parry 9; Raff 35; Rheinberger 18; Rimsky-Korsakov 13; Rossini 65; Saint-Saëns 22; Smetana 33; Spohr 73; Stainer 17; Stanford 5; Johann Strauss 32; Sullivan 15; Tchaikovsky 17; Verdi 44; Wagner 44; S. S. Wesley 47.

Year	Age	Life	Contemporary Musicians
1858	1		Leoncavallo born, March 8; Puccini born, June 22; Ethel Smyth born, April 23.
1859	2	Family moves back into Worcester. Brother, Joe, born.	Spohr (75) dies, Oct. 22.
1860	3		Albéniz born, May 29; Charpentier born, June 25; Mahler born, July 7; Wolf born, March 13.
1861	4	Brother, Frank, born.	Arensky born, Aug. 11; MacDowell born, Dec. 18; Marschner (66) dies, Dec. 14.
1862	5		Debussy born, Aug. 22; Delius born, Jan. 29; E. German born, Feb. 17; Halévy (63) dies, March 17.
1863	6		Mascagni born, Dec. 7; Somervell born, June 5.
1864	7	Goes to school. Sister Helen (Dot) born. Brother Harry dies of scarlet fever.	Meyerbeer (72) dies, May 2; Richard Strauss born, June 11.
1865	8		Dukas born, Oct. 1; Glazunov born, Aug. 10; Sibelius born, Dec. 8; Nielsen born, June 9.
1866	9	Helps in father's shop in Worcester. Brother Joe dies.	Busoni born, April 1; Satie born, May 17.
1867	10	First known composition, 'Fairies and Giants' (later used in *Wand of Youth* Suite)	Granados born, July 27.
1868	11	Attends Littleton House school.	Bantock born, Aug. 7; Berwald (71) dies, April 3; Rossini (76) dies, Nov. 13.
1869	12	He learns to play violin, viola, cello and bassoon as well as piano and organ.	Berlioz (65) dies, March 8; Dargomizhsky (55) dies, Jan. 17; Walford Davies born, Sept. 6; Roussel born, April 5.

Appendix A—Calendar

Year	Age	Life	Contemporary Musicians
1870	13		Balfe (62) dies, Oct. 20; Lekeu born, Jan. 20; Novák born, Dec. 5; Florent Schmitt born, Sept. 28.
1871	14		Auber (89) dies, May 12.
1872	15	Song, 'The Language of Flowers'. Apprenticed to solicitor, but gives up after about a year.	Skriabin born, Jan. 6; Vaughan Williams born, Oct. 12.
1873	16	Assistant organist at St George's Roman Catholic Church.	Rakhmaninov born, April 1; Reger born, March 19.
1874	17	Violinist in orchestra of Worcester Festival Choral Society.	Holst born, Sept. 21; Schönberg born, Sept. 13; Suk born, Jan. 4.
1875	18		Sterndale Bennett (59) dies, Feb. 1; Bizet (36) dies, June 3; Coleridge-Taylor born, Aug 15; Ravel born, March 7.
1876	19		Falla born, Nov. 23; S. S. Wesley (66) dies, April 19.
1877	20	Violin lessons with Adolphe Pollitzer in London.	Dohnányi born, July 27; Dunhill born, Feb. 1; Quilter born, Nov. 1.
1878	21		Boughton born, Jan. 23; Holbrooke born, July 6.
1879	22	Appointed Band Instructor to the County and City of Worcester Pauper Lunatic Asylum at Powick. Sister Pollie married to William Grafton.	Frank Bridge born, Feb. 26; Ireland born, Aug. 13; Respighi born, July 9; Cyril Scott born, Sept. 20.
1880	23		Bloch born, July 24; Medtner born, Jan. 5; Offenbach (61) dies, Oct. 5; Pizzetti born, Sept. 20.

Year	Age	Life	Contemporary Musicians
1881	24	Sister Lucy married to Charles Pipe.	Bartók born, March 25; Mussorgsky (42) dies, March 28.
1882	25		Kodály born, Dec. 16; Malipiero born, March 18; Raff (60) dies, June 24–5; Stravinsky born, June 17; Szymanowski born, Oct. 6.
1883	26	'Intermezzo Moresque' (later 'Sérénade Mauresque', Op. 10, No. 2) performed by W. C. Stockley's Birmingham Orchestra.	Bax born, Nov. 8; Berners born, Sept. 18; Casella born, July 25; Wagner (69) dies, Feb. 13; Webern born, Dec. 3.
1884	27	Resigns from asylum post.	van Dieren born, Dec. 27; Griffes born, Sept. 17; Smetana (60) dies, May 12.
1885	28	Organist at St George's Roman Catholic church.	Berg born, Feb. 9; Varèse born, Dec. 22; Wellesz born, Oct. 21.
1886	29	Caroline Alice Roberts (born Oct. 9, 1848) first becomes pupil.	Liszt (74) dies, July 31.
1887	30		Borodin (53) dies, Feb. 28; Villa-Lobos born, March 5.
1888	31		Durey born, May 27.
1889	32	Marries Caroline Alice Roberts at Brompton Oratory. They move to London. *Liebesgruss* (later *Salut d'Amour*) published.	Shaporin born, Nov. 8.
1890	33	*Froissart* first performed at Worcester Festival. Daughter Carice Irene, born Aug. 14.	Franck (67) dies, Nov. 8; Gade (73) dies, Dec. 21.
1891	34	Still virtually unknown as a composer, settles in Malvern.	Bliss born, Aug. 2; Delibes (54) dies, Jan. 16; Prokofiev born, April 23.
1892	35		Honegger born, March 10; Howells born, Oct. 17; Kilpinen born, Feb. 4; Lalo

Year	Age	Life	Contemporary Musicians
			(69) dies, April 22; Milhaud born, Sept. 4; Sorabji born, Aug. 14.
1893	36	*The Black Knight* performed at Worcester.	Eugene Goossens born, May 26; Gounod (75) dies, Oct. 18; Hába born, June 21; Tchaikovsky (53) dies, Nov. 6.
1894	37		Chabrier (53) dies, Sept. 13; Lekeu (24) dies, Jan. 21; Moeran born, Dec. 31; Pijper born, Sept. 8; Warlock born, Oct. 30.
1895	38	Composes Organ Sonata, Op. 28.	Hindemith born, Nov. 16.
1896	39	*From the Bavarian Highlands* and *Lux Christi* (*The Light of Life*) performed at Worcester. *King Olaf* performed at Hanley.	Bruckner (72) dies, Oct. 11; Sessions born, Dec. 28.
1897	40	*Imperial March* and *The Banner of St George* composed for Queen Victoria's Diamond Jubilee.	Brahms (63) dies, April 3.
1898	41	First performance of *Caractacus*, Leeds.	Roy Harris born, Feb. 12.
1899	42	First performances of the *Enigma Variations*, London, and *Sea Pictures*, Norwich.	Auric born, Feb. 15; Chausson (44) dies, June 10; Johann Strauss (73) dies, June 3.
1900	43	*The Dream of Gerontius* first performed at Birmingham, without success. Hon. Mus.D., Cambridge.	Copland born, Nov. 14; Křenek born, Aug. 23; Sullivan (58) dies, Nov. 22.
1901	44	First performance of *Cockaigne*, London. *Gerontius* performed at Lower Rhine	Rheinberger (62) dies, Nov. 25; Finzi born, July 14; Rubbra born, May 23;

Year	Age	Life	Contemporary Musicians
		Festival, Düsseldorf, with success.	Stainer (61) dies, March 31; Verdi (87) dies, Jan. 27.
1902	45	Mother's death, Sept. 1.	Walton born, March 29.
1903	46	*The Apostles* first performed at Birmingham.	Berkeley born, May 12; Blacher born, Jan. 3; Wolf (42) dies, Feb. 22.
1904	47	Knighted July 5. Overture *In the South* first performed in Elgar Festival, Covent Garden.	Dallapiccola born, Feb. 3; Dvořák (62) dies, May 1.
1905	48	Professorship at Birmingham University. Visit to U.S.A. *Introduction and Allegro* first performed, London.	Constant Lambert born, Aug. 23; Tippett born, Jan. 2.
1906	49	Father's death, April 30. *The Kingdom* first performed at Birmingham.	Shostakovich born, Sept. 25.
1907	50		Grieg (63) dies, Sept. 4.
1908	51	First performance of Symphony No. 1 in Manchester.	MacDowell (46) dies, Jan. 23; Rimsky-Korsakov (64) dies, June 21; Messiaen born, Dec. 10; William B. Wordsworth born, Dec. 17.
1909	52		Albéniz (48) dies, May 18.
1910	53	First performance of Violin Concerto in London, with Kreisler as soloist.	Balakirev (73) dies, May 29; Samuel Barber born, March 9; William Schuman born, Aug. 4.
1911	54	First performance of Symphony No. 2 in London. O.M. conferred.	Mahler (50) dies, May 18.
1912	55	*The Music Makers* first performed at Birmingham.	Coleridge-Taylor (37) dies, Sept. 1; Massenet (70) dies, Aug. 13.
1913	56	*Falstaff* first performed at Leeds.	Britten born, Nov. 22.
1914	57		Liadov (59) dies, Aug. 28.

Year	Age	Life	Contemporary Musicians
1915	58	Incidental music to *The Starlight Express*.	Skriabin (43) dies, April 27. Searle born Aug. 26.
1916	59		Granados (48) dies, March 24; Reger (43) dies, May 11; Parrott born, March 5.
1917	60	All three parts of *The Spirit of England* first performed at Albert Hall, London.	
1918	61		Boito (76) dies, June 10; Cui (83) dies, March 24; Debussy (55) dies, March 25; Parry (70) dies, Oct. 7.
1919	62	First performances of Violin Sonata, String Quartet, Piano Quintet and Cello Concerto, London.	Leoncavallo (61) dies, Aug. 9.
1920	63	His wife (71) dies, April 7.	Bruch (82) dies, Oct. 2; Griffes (36) dies, April 8.
1921	64		Humperdinck (67) dies, Sept. 27; Saint-Saëns (86) dies, Dec. 16.
1922	65		Lukas Foss born, Aug. 15.
1923	66		
1924	67	Appointed Master of the King's Musick.	Busoni (58) dies, July 27; Fauré (79) dies, Nov. 4; Puccini (65) dies, Nov. 29; Stanford (71) dies, March 29.
1925	68	Receives Gold Medal of Royal Philharmonic Society, Nov. 19. Sister Lucy dies.	Boulez born, March 25; Satie (59) dies, July 1.
1926	69		Henze born, July 1.
1927	70		
1928	71	K.C.V.O. Brother Frank dies.	Janáček (74) dies, Aug. 12.
1929	72		
1930	73	*Severn Suite* first performed at	Warlock (36) dies, Dec. 17.

Appendix A—Calendar

Year	Age	Life	Contemporary Musicians
		Crystal Palace Brass Band Festival.	
1931	74	Created baronet.	d'Indy (80) dies, Dec. 2; Nielsen (66) dies, Oct. 2.
1932	75	Works on sketches for an opera, *The Spanish Lady*.	
1933	76	Works on sketches for Symphony No. 3. First signs of illness. G.C.V.O.	Duparc (85) dies, Feb. 13.
1934	76	Dies at Worcester, Feb. 23.	Delius (72) dies, June 10; Holst (59) dies, May 25; Auric 35; Bantock 66; Barber 24; Bartók 53; Bax 51; Berg 49; Berkeley 31; Berners 51; Blacher 31; Bliss 43; Bloch 54; Boughton 56; Boulez 9; Frank Bridge 55; Britten 21; Casella 51; Charpentier 74; Copland 34; Cowen 82; Dallapiccola 30; Walford Davies 65; van Dieren 50; Dohnányi 57; Dukas 69; Dunhill 57; Durey 46; Falla 58; Lukas Foss 12; German 72; Glazunov 69; Goossens 41; Hába 41; Roy Harris 36; Henze 8; Hindemith 39; Honegger 42; Howells 42; Ireland 55; Kodály 52; Křenek 34; Lambert 29; McEwen 66; Mackenzie 87; Malipiero 52; Mascagni 71; Medtner 54; Messiaen 26; Milhaud 42; Moeran 40; Novák 64; Parrott 18; Pijper 40; Pizzetti 54; Poulenc 35; Proko-

Year	Age	Life	Contemporary Musicians

fiev 43; Quilter 57; Rakh-maninov 61; Ravel 59; Respighi 55; Roussel 65; Rubbra 33; Florent Schmitt 64; Schönberg 60; William Schuman 24; Cyril Scott 55; Searle 19; Sessions 38; Shaporin 45; Shostakovich 28; Sibelius 69; Ethel Smyth 75; Somervell 71; Sorabji 42; Richard Strauss 70; Stravinsky 52; Suk 60; Szymanowski 51: Tippett 29; Varèse 49; Vaughan Williams 62; Villa-Lobos 47; Walton 32; Webern 51; Wellesz 49.

APPENDIX B

CATALOGUE OF WORKS

ORCHESTRAL WORKS

Op.		Date
1A	*The Wand of Youth*. First Suite	1867–1907
1B	*The Wand of Youth*. Second Suite	1879–1908
3	*Cantique*	1879–1912
7	*Sevillaña* (Scène Espagnole)	1884–9
10	*Three Pieces for Small Orchestra*	1882–8
	1. Mazurka	
	2. Sérénade Mauresque	
	3. Contrasts	
11	*Sursum Corda* (brass, organ and strings)	1894
12	*Salut d'Amour* (*Liebesgruss*)	1888
	(also many arrangements)	
19	*Froissart*. Concert overture	1890
20	*Serenade*. Strings	1892
32	*Imperial March*	1897
36	*Variations on an Original Theme* (Enigma)	1898–9
39	*Pomp and Circumstance*. Marches	1901–30
	1. D ma 1901 2. A mi 1901	
	3. C mi 1904 4. G ma 1907	
	5. C ma 1930	
40	*Cockaigne*. Overture	1901
43	*Dream Children*. Two pieces for piano or small orchestra	1902
47	*Introduction and Allegro*. String quartet and string orchestra	1901–5
50	*In the South* (Alassio). Overture	1899–1904
55	Symphony No. 1 in A flat ma	1907–8
58	*Elegy*. String orchestra	1909
63	Symphony No. 2 in E flat ma	1903–10
65	*Coronation March*	1902–11
68	*Falstaff*. Symphonic Study	1902–13

Appendix B—Catalogue of Works

Op.		Date
70	*Sospiri.* Strings, harp and organ	1914
75	*Carillon.* Reciter and orchestra	1914
76	*Polonia.* Symphonic prelude	1915
77	*Une Voix dans le Désert.* Reciter and orchestra	1915
79	*Le Drapeau Belge.* Reciter and orchestra	1917
87	*Severn Suite.* Brass band	1930
	Arranged for orchestra	1932
	Arranged by Ivor Atkins for organ (Sonata No. 2)	1933
88	Symphony No. 3. Fragments only	1933
—	*Rosemary*	1882
—	*Sérénade Lyrique*	1899
—	*Carissima*	1914
—	*Nursery Suite*	1931
—	*Mina.* Small orchestra	1934

INCIDENTAL MUSIC

42	*Grania and Diarmid* (George Moore and W. B. Yeats). Funeral March, song and incidental music	1901
66	*The Crown of India.* Masque in 12 movements for 6 soloists, chorus and orchestra (Henry Hamilton)	1902–12
78	*The Starlight Express* (play by Violet Pearn based on book, *A Prisoner in Fairyland,* by Algernon Blackwood)	1915
81	*The Sanguine Fan.* Ballet	1917
—	*The Fringes of the Fleet.* Four songs by Kipling and one by Gilbert Parker	1917
—	*King Arthur.* (L. Binyon) MS.	1923
—	*Pageant of Empire* for Wembley Exhibition in 8 movements	1924
—	*Beau Brummel.* (Bertram P. Matthews) MS.	1928

SOLO INSTRUMENT AND ORCHESTRA

61	Concerto for Violin in B mi	1909–10
62	*Romance for Bassoon*	1910
85	Concerto for Violoncello in E mi	1919
90	Concerto for Piano. Fragments only	1909–32

Appendix B—Catalogue of Works

Appendix B—Catalogue of Works

Op.		Date
—	Piece for Organ. MS. 'For Dot's nuns'	1906
—	*Sonatina.* Piano	before 1932
—	*Adieu.* Piano (transcribed for violin by Szigeti)	before 1932
—	*Serenade.* Piano (transcribed for violin by Szigeti)	before 1932

SONGS

5	'A War Song' ('A Soldier's Song') (C. F. Hayward)	1884
16	1. 'Shepherd's Song' (Barry Pain)	1892
	2. 'Through the Long Days' (John Hay)	1885
	3. 'Rondel' (Longfellow from Froissart)	1894
31	1. 'After' (Philip Bourke Marston)	1895
	2. 'A Song of Flight' (Christina Rossetti)	before 1900
37	*Sea Pictures.* Contralto and orchestra	1897–9
	1. 'Sea Slumber Song' (Hon. Roden Noel)	
	2. 'In Haven' ('Love alone will stay') (C. Alice Elgar)	
	3. 'Sabbath Morning at Sea' (Elizabeth Barrett Browning)	
	4. 'Where Corals Lie' (Richard Garnett)	
	5. 'The Swimmer' (Adam Lindsay Gordon)	
41	1. 'In the Dawn' (A. C. Benson)	before 1901
	2. 'Speak, Music' (A. C. Benson)	
48	'Pleading' (Arthur L. Salmon) (also with orchestra)	before 1908
59	Song cycle with orchestra (Nos. 1, 2 and 4 not composed) (Gilbert Parker)	1909–10
	3. 'Oh! Soft was the song'	
	5. 'Was it some golden star?'	
	6. 'Twilight'	
60	Folk Songs (from Eastern Europe) (Pietro d'Alba) with orchestra	
	1. 'The Torch'	1909
	2. 'The River'	1910
—	'The Language of Flowers' (Percival)	1872
—	'Is she not passing fair?' (Charles, Duke of Orléans, trans. Louisa Stuart Costello)	1886

Appendix B—Catalogue of Works

Op.		Date
—	'As I laye a-thinking' (Thomas Ingoldsby)	*c.* 1888
—	'The Wind at Dawn' (C. Alice Roberts)	1888
—	'Queen Mary's Song' (Tennyson)	1889
—	'Like to the Damask Rose' (Simon Wastell)	1892
—	'A Song of Autumn' (A. Lindsay Gordon)	1892
—	'The Poet's Life' (Ellen Burroughs)	1892
—	'Love alone will stay'. See *Sea Pictures*, No. 2	1898
—	'Dry those fair, those crystal eyes' (Henry King)	1899
—	'Pipes of Pan' (Adrian Ross)	*c.* 1899
—	'Come, gentle night' (Clifton Bingham)	*c.* 1901
—	'Always and everywhere' (Krasinski, trans. F. E. Fortey)	*c.* 1901
—	'Land of Hope and Glory' (A. C. Benson, arranged from *Coronation Ode*)	?1901
—	'Speak, my heart' (A. C. Benson)	?1902
—	'The Kingsway' (C. Alice Elgar)	1909
—	'A Child Asleep' (Elizabeth Barrett Browning)	1909
—	'Arabian Serenade' (Margery Lawrence)	before 1914
—	'The Chariots of the Lord' (John Brownlie)	1914
—	'Fight for Right' (William Morris)	1916
—	'Big Steamers' (Rudyard Kipling)	1918
—	'It isnae me' (Sally Holmes)	1930
—	Unison songs (words by Charles Mackay):	
	'The Rapid Stream' (also 2-part, 1933)	1932
	'When Swallows fly'	1932
	'The Woodland Stream' (also 2-part, 1933)	1933

CHORAL MUSIC

Cantatas, Oratorios and Odes, etc.

25	*The Black Knight* (Uhland trans. Longfellow)	1890–2
27	*From the Bavarian Highlands* (C. Alice Elgar); also for orchestra alone (3 Dances)	1895
29	*The Light of Life* (*Lux Christi*) (E. Capel-Cure)	1896
30	Scenes from the *Saga of King Olaf* (Longfellow and H. A. Acworth)	1894–6
33	*The Banner of St George* (Shapcott Wensley)	*c.* 1897
35	*Caractacus* (H. A. Acworth)	1897–8

Appendix B—Catalogue of Works

Op.		Date
38	*The Dream of Gerontius* (John Henry Newman)	1899–1900
44	*Coronation Ode* (A. C. Benson)	1901–2
49	*The Apostles* (Elgar)	1902–3
51	*The Kingdom* (Elgar)	1905–6
69	*The Music Makers* (Arthur O'Shaughnessy)	?1902–12
80	*The Spirit of England* (Laurence Binyon)	
	1. 'The Fourth of August'	1917
	2. 'To Women'	1915
	3. 'For the Fallen'	1915

Church Music

2	1. *Ave Verum Corpus*	1887
	2. *Ave Maria*	
	3. *Ave Maris Stella*	
	Also with English words for C. of E.	
34	*Te Deum* and *Benedictus*	1897
64	*Coronation Offertorium*, 'O hearken thou'	1911
67	'Great is the Lord' (Psalm 48)	1912
74	'Give unto the Lord' (Psalm 29)	1914
—	Music for St George's Roman Catholic Church	*c.* 1875–85
—	*O Salutaris Hostia* (4-part)	*c.* 1880
—	*O Salutaris Hostia* (Tozer's *Benediction Manual*)	before 1898
—	*Ecce Sacerdos Magnus*	1888
—	'Lo! Christ the Lord is born'. Carol (Shapcott Wensley)	*c* 1897
—	'O mightiest of the mighty.' Hymn (S. Childs Clarke)	*c.* 1901
—	Two Single Chants and Two Double Chants	1909
—	'They are at rest.' Elegy (John Henry Newman)	1909
—	'Fear not, O land.' Harvest anthem	1914
—	'I sing the birth.' Carol (Ben Jonson)	1928
—	'Good morrow.' Carol (George Gascoigne)	1929

Part-songs (accompanied)

23	'Spanish Serenade' ('Stars of the summer night': Longfellow). With orchestra	1891

Op.		Date
26	For women's voices with 2 vi. and piano (C. Alice Elgar):	1894
	1. 'The Snow'	
	2. 'Fly, singing bird'	
52	'A Christmas Greeting' (C. Alice Elgar)	1907
	2 sop., male chorus ad lib., 2 vi. and pf.	

PART-SONGS (unaccompanied)

(for mixed voices unless otherwise indicated)

18	1. 'O happy eyes' (C. Alice Elgar)	1890
	2. 'Love' (Arthur Maquarie)	1890
45	*Part-songs from the Greek Anthology* for male voices	1902
	1. 'Yea, cast me from heights' (trans. Alma Strettell)	
	2. 'Whether I find thee' (trans. Andrew Lang)	
	3. 'After many a dusty mile' (trans. Edmund Gosse)	
	4. 'It's oh, to be a wild wind' (trans. W. M. Hardinge)	
	5. 'Feasting I watch' (trans. Richard Garnett)	
53	Four Part-songs	1907
	1. 'There is sweet music' (Tennyson)	
	2. 'Deep in my soul' (Byron)	
	3. 'O wild west wind' (Shelley)	
	4. 'Owls' (an epitaph) (Elgar)	
54	'The Reveille', male voices (Bret Harte)	1907
56	'Angelus (Tuscany)' (from the Tuscan)	1909
57	'Go, song of mine,' 6 parts (Calvacanti, trans. Rossetti)	1909
71	Two Part-songs (Henry Vaughan)	before 1914
	1. 'The Shower'	
	2. 'The Fountain'	
72	'Death on the Hills' (Maikov, trans. Rosa Newmarch)	1914
73	Two Part-songs (Maikov, trans. Rosa Newmarch)	1914
	1. 'Love's Tempest'	
	2. 'Serenade'	

Appendix B—Catalogue of Works

Op.		Date
—	'My love dwelt in a northern land' (Andrew Lang)	1890
—	'Grete Malverne on a Rock'	1897
—	'To her beneath whose steadfast star' (F. W. H. Myers)	1899
—	'Weary wind of the west' (T. E. Brown)	1903
—	'Evening Scene' (Coventry Patmore)	1905
—	'How calmly the evening' (T. T. Lynch)	1907
—	'The Birthright' (George A. Stocks)	c. 1914
—	'Marching Song' (Capt. de Courcy Stretton)	c. 1908
	(also for male voices as 'Follow the colours')	1914
—	'The Wanderer', male voices (from *Wit and Drollery*, 1661)	c. 1923
—	'Zut, zut, zut', male voices (Richard Marden)	c. 1923
—	'The Herald', male voices (Alexander Smith)	c. 1925
—	'The Prince of Sleep' (Walter de la Mare)	c. 1925

OPERA

89	*The Spanish Lady* (Ben Jonson adapted by Elgar and Barry Jackson). Planned in two acts, but incomplete.	1878–1933

ARRANGEMENTS

—	Orchestration of *Emmaus* by Herbert Brewer	published 1901
—	'God Save the King', soloists, chorus and orch.	published 1902
—	Edition of *St Matthew Passion* by Bach with Ivor Atkins	published 1911
—	Chorales from above arrangement for 3 tpts., 4 hns., 3 tbnes. and tuba	MS. 1911
86	Fantasia and Fugue in C mi by Bach, arranged for full orchestra	1921–2
—	Toccata in F by Bach, arranged Esser, rearranged Elgar	?
—	Orchestration of 'Jerusalem' by Parry	MS. 1922
—	Orchestration of *Jehova quam multi sunt* by Purcell	MS. 1929
—	Overture in D mi by Handel, arranged for full orchestra	published 1923

Appendix B—Catalogue of Works

— Funeral March by Chopin, arranged for full
orchestra   published 1933

Juvenilia include paraphrase of Mozart's Symphony in G mi (1878); and arrangements of
Beethoven (1880) and Wagner, part of *Tannhäuser* for piano (1883) and Good Friday music
from *Parsifal* for small orchestra (1894)

Also orchestrations of works by S. S. Wesley,
Battishill, hymns, etc.

WRITINGS

Programme notes for Worcestershire Phil. Soc.	1898–1904
Preface to *The Singing of the Future* by D. Ffrangcon-Davies	1904
Lectures, Birmingham University	1905–6
'Analytical Notes on *Falstaff*', *Musical Times*	1913
My Friends Pictured Within	1913
'Gray, Walpole, West and Ashton', *Times Literary Supplement*	4 Sept. 1919
'Notation', *Musical Times*	1920
'Scott and Shakespeare', *Times Literary Supplement*	21 July 1921
Foreword to *Forgotten Worcester* by H. A. Leicester	1930

APPENDIX C

PERSONALIA

Allen, Sir Hugh Percy (1869–1946), born at Reading, organ scholar of Christ's College, Cambridge, organist at various cathedrals; a bluff, vigorous and generous character. He left little in writing, but his many friends and pupils have testified to his varied enthusiasms in music and musicians, and his influence was considerable. In 1918 he combined the post of Director of the Royal College of Music with the Chair of Music at Oxford and two years later was knighted. Sir Thomas Armstrong delivered an informative centenary address at Oxford in June 1969.

Atkins, Sir Ivor Algernon (1869–1953), from 1897 to 1950 organist at Worcester Cathedral and Three Choirs Festival conductor, he was knighted in 1921. A composer, he collaborated with Elgar in preparing a new edition of Bach's *St Matthew Passion*.

Bantock, Sir Granville (1868–1946), born in London, a prolific composer whose larger scores include the complicated *Omar Khayyám*, he succeeded Elgar as Peyton Professor of Music at Birmingham University in 1908. He also ran the School of Music in Birmingham until 1934 and later became chairman of the corporation of Trinity College of Music, London. He was knighted in 1930.

Blake, Mrs Carice Irene (1890–1970, née Elgar), Elgar's only child, she was educated in Malvern and Italy. Married in 1922 to Samuel Blake (d. 1939), she helped her father in many ways after the death of Lady Elgar and for many years had a great deal to do with looking after the Birthplace Museum at Broadheath.

Broadhurst, Edgar C. (1877–1967), chorister at Hereford Choir School at the age of seven; Dr Sinclair's assistant at Hereford Cathedral from 1892. He was appointed organist at St Michael's College, Tenbury, in 1896. From 1907 to 1947 he was Assistant Music Master at Harrow School and organist of Harrow parish church. In 1952 he became organist at St George's Church, Worcester.

Appendix C—Personalia

Buths, Julius (1851–1920), German conductor in Düsseldorf from 1890; directed the Lower Rhine Festival there, where he introduced Elgar's *Gerontius* in December 1901 and again in May 1902.

Cohen, Harriet (1895–1967), pianist, famous for being a champion of modern British music, especially that of Bax; she recorded with the Stratton Quartet the Elgar Piano Quintet and in spite of a severe hand injury received in 1948 played the slow movement of Elgar's unfinished Piano Concerto with the Boyd Neel Orchestra in 1956. During the last seven years of her life she devoted much time to her Harriet Cohen International Awards for composers, performers and music scholars.

Colvin, Sir Sidney (1845–1927), a great personal friend of the Elgars, he was appointed Keeper of the Department of Prints and Drawings at the British Museum in 1884 and was knighted in 1911. The Cello Concerto was dedicated to him and his wife. They lived near the Elgars in Sussex at that time.

Davies, Sir Henry Walford (1869–1941), organist at the Temple, then Professor of Music at the University College of Wales, Aberystwyth, from 1919 to 1926, made Master of the King's Musick on the death of Elgar; popularizer of music, he was famous for his broadcast talks in the twenties and thirties. In the early days of the century his music, taken up by Wood at the Proms and by other organizations including the Three Choirs Festival, was thought to be important—the Novello printing may have helped. Now the pretentious works have faded and only miniatures such as the *Solemn Melody* and 'God be in My Head' remain.

Griffith, Arthur Troyte (1864–1942), of Welsh extraction, No. 7 in the *Enigma Variations*, a Malvern architect and water-colourist, he was a life-long friend and correspondent of Elgar (see also in Chapter VII).

Hall, Marie (1884–1956), a violinist who made her début in Prague in 1902; in 1916 she was the first soloist to record Elgar's Violin Concerto. The Stradivarius violin which she bought in 1905 for £1,600 was sold at Sotheby's in 1968 for £22,000 (*The Times*, 8th November 1968). Married in 1911 to Edward Baring. Vaughan Williams wrote *The Lark Ascending* for her.

Hull, Sir Percy Clarke (1878–1968), in 1896 succeeded Broadhurst as Dr Sinclair's assistant at Hereford Cathedral. As a prisoner of war in

Germany, he was in the same internment camp as fellow-musicians Benjamin Dale (1885–1943), composer, and Arthur Williams (1875–1939), the cellist of whom Elgar spoke highly as soloist in his Cello Concerto in 1924. He was organist of Hereford from 1918 until 1949 and knighted in 1947.

Jaeger, August Johannes (1860–1909), from Düsseldorf, No. 9 in the *Enigma Variations* and one of Elgar's greatest inspirers. A dozen years after his arrival in England, he joined the firm of Novello in 1890 and, although in a junior position, he became chief negotiator between Elgar and the firm, as well as an enthusiastic private correspondent and writer of analytical notes (see also in Chapter VII).

Kreisler, Fritz (1875–1962), Viennese violinist, made his London debut with Richter in 1901 and received the gold medal of the Royal Philharmonic Society in 1904. He gave the first performance in 1910 of Elgar's Violin Concerto, which was dedicated to him. His own compositions, mainly trifles imitated from light classical models, were very popular when brilliantly performed by himself.

Maine, Rev. Basil Stephen (b. 1894), from Norwich, a music critic and author who wrote two volumes on Elgar, one on his life and one on his work, both published in 1933. He was ordained in 1939.

Manns, Sir August (1825–1907), from Germany, became first sub-conductor and then, in 1855, conductor to the Crystal Palace Company (Secretary: Sir George Grove), converting a brass band into a full symphony orchestra. He introduced to London the music of Sullivan in 1862 and that of Elgar in 1884.

Menuhin, Yehudi (b. 1916), American-born Jewish concert violinist of distinction, he was associated with Elgar's Violin Concerto first as a boy of fifteen. Resident in London since 1960, he founded the Yehudi Menuhin School for musically gifted children in 1964 and was made an Honorary Knight Commander of the Most Excellent Order of the British Empire in 1965. Festivals in many places from Bath to Gstaad have owed much to his direction.

Newman, Ernest (1868–1959), one of the most famous music critics of his time, he was first noticed in Liverpool where he met Elgar in 1900. He was critic of the *Manchester Guardian* in 1905, the *Birmingham Post* in 1906, the *Observer* in 1919 and then for many years from 1920 the *Sunday Times*. He wrote books and programme notes about many composers, including Elgar, but his greatest achievement was the four volumes on the life of Wagner (completed in 1947). His critical writings on Elgar were frequently frankly harsh but the Piano Quintet's dedication to him proved a personal friendship.

Norbury, the sisters *Florence* (1858–1937) and *Winifred* (1861–1938), both commemorated in the *Enigma Variations* (see Chapter VII) though only the latter's initials appear at the head of the movement. They lived at Sherridge, adjoining Birchwood, which Elgar used as a summer cottage from 1898 to 1903. Winifred helped with the copying of parts on several occasions. She was also Joint Secretary of the Worcestershire Philharmonic Society.

Parry, Sir C. Hubert H. (1848–1918), an important English composer who succeeded Sir George Grove as Director of the Royal College of Music in 1894 and six years later became also Professor of Music at Oxford University. One of his best-known works is *Blest Pair of Sirens.* Elgar came to know his music when performed at the Three Choirs Festival and he orchestrated 'Jerusalem' for the Leeds Festival of 1922.

Pollitzer, Adolf (1832–1900), Hungarian violinist, with whom Elgar studied as a young man; he came to London in 1851 and led first the orchestra of Her Majesty's Theatre, then that of the New Philharmonic Society and then that of the Royal Choral Society. He introduced Elgar to Manns (q.v.).

Powell, Mrs Richard (1874–1964, née Dora Mary Penny), of Wolverhampton, No. 10, 'Dorabella', of the *Enigma Variations,* first met Elgar in 1895. A woman of strong views, author in 1936 of *Edward Elgar: Memories of a Variation,* in characteristic vein she wrote to Mr E. A. Butcher in March 1955: 'Did you hear M. Sargent *dirge* "Nimrod" the other night? It made me ill! Yes, and then he plays "Troyte" like a whirlwind. . . .' She was inclined to over-emphasize the happy side of Elgar (see also in Chapter VII).

Reed, William Henry (1876–1942), violinist who studied at the Royal Academy of Music, and became leader of the London Symphony Orchestra in 1912. He helped Elgar with the Violin Concerto and the chamber music, playing over much of the music while it was still in only sketch form. A great personal friend of the composer, he played in many performances and wrote two books on him.

Richter, Hans (1843–1916), Austro-Hungarian conductor who studied in Vienna, where he was a horn player at the opera. First to conduct Wagner's *Ring* at Bayreuth in 1876, he came to London the following year. From 1897 to 1911 conductor of the Hallé Orchestra in Manchester, he was a great champion of Elgar, whose Symphony No. 1 was dedicated to him, 'true artist and true friend'.

Ronald, Sir Landon (1873–1938), London-born conductor who became an important interpreter of Elgar's music. 'He wants to make more of every passage than you do', wrote Bernard Shaw to Elgar on 7th January 1932. Principal of the Guildhall School of Music from 1910 to 1937, Landon Ronald was knighted in 1922.

Schuster, Leo Francis (Frank) Howard (1852–1927), of German-Jewish extraction, a patron of the arts. He and his sister Adela entertained various artists at 'The Hut' at Bray, three miles from Maidenhead, and took considerable interest in Elgar. Another friend of similar blood and wealth was *Alfred Rodewald* (d. 1903), a Liverpool businessman, who had a villa at Betws-y-Coed, in North Wales, called Minafon, where Elgar wrote some of *The Apostles*.

Shaw, George Bernard (1856–1950), great Irish playwright and also a most discerning critic of music, as his observations on London concerts in the eighties and nineties show. While Elgar grew to like his plays, Shaw in his turn became an enthusiast for Elgar's symphonic works. The *Severn Suite* was dedicated to him.

Sinclair, George Robertson (1862–1917), Irish musician, No. 11 in the *Enigma Variations*. After being assistant conductor at Gloucester Cathedral, he was appointed organist at the Cathedral of Truro in 1880 and at that of Hereford in 1889. He had a strong influence in widening the repertoire of the Three Choirs Festival. Between 1897 and 1903, Elgar wrote 'The Moods of Dan, Illustrated' in his Visitors' Book. Although ostensibly referring to Sinclair's bulldog, some of these seven musical snippets anticipated motives in *Gerontius*, *In the South, The Apostles* and *For the Fallen* (see also in Chapter VII). Dan is buried in Hereford Conservative Club garden.

Stanford, Sir Charles Villiers (1852–1924), Irish composer who, with Parry, was considered to have helped bring about a 'renaissance' in British music. Elgar and Stanford did not always get on together but the latter, as Professor of Music at Cambridge from 1887, did see that the former was awarded an honorary doctorate in 1900. Later he had Elgar nominated for membership of the Athenaeum.

Strauss, Richard (1864–1949), Munich-born composer, at one time considered to be Elgar's greatest contemporary. Elgar met him at Garmisch in 1897. After the repeat performance of *Gerontius* at Düsseldorf in 1902, Strauss toasted Elgar as the 'first English progressive musician'. Elgar's orchestration of the Fugue (1921) and Fantasia (1922) in C minor of Bach was said to be the outcome of a wager with Strauss, who, like Elgar, was admired for his masterly orchestration.

Stuart of Wortley, Lady (Alice Stuart-Wortley, 1862–1936), third daughter of Sir John Millais. Her husband, Charles Stuart-Wortley, was created Baron in 1916. A friendship with Elgar grew from his visits to Sheffield and developed in London. A considerable correspondence, starting in about 1903, lasted for more than twenty years. Musical and sympathetic, she was involved to some extent in inspiring the composition of parts of Symphony No. 2 and more particularly the Violin Concerto.

Wood, Sir Henry Joseph (1869–1944), London-born conductor, became famous for his Promenade Concerts which started at the Queen's Hall in 1895. 'I suppose there will be a chance for English composers some day at Queen's Hall', wrote Jaeger to Elgar on 8th March 1898. The 'Meditation' from *The Light of Life* was given in May the following year and later Wood took up Elgar's music with enthusiasm. The *Grania and Diarmid* music is dedicated to this conductor, who did much for many living British composers in his time.

Young, Dr Percy Marshall (b. Cheshire, 1912), author on various subjects, was educated at Christ's Hospital and Cambridge. Director of Music at Wolverhampton College of Technology from 1945 to 1966 and expert on football. Young has written on many composers but has made a speciality of Elgar. Also a composer and recently appointed adviser on music in Nigeria, he published a substantial *History of British Music* in 1967. Songs and a string orchestra suite from Elgar's unfinished opera, *The Spanish Lady*, have been edited and published by him.

APPENDIX D

BIBLIOGRAPHY

Anderson, W. R., 'Introduction to the Music of Elgar' (London, 1949).

Barber, Cecil, 'Enigma Variations: the Original Finale' (*Music and Letters,* April 1935).

Bax, Sir Arnold, 'Farewell my Youth' (London, 1943).

Bennett, Joseph, '*King Olaf,* Analytical Notes' (London, 1896).

Bonavia, Ferruccio, 'Elgar' in *Lives of the Great Composers,* vol. iii (London, 1935), *The Symphony* (ed. Ralph Hill, London, 1949), and *The Music Makers,* vol. iii (London, 1952).

Brent Smith, A. E., 'The Humour of Elgar' (*Music and Letters,* January 1935).

Buckley, R. J., 'Sir Edward Elgar' in *Living Masters of Music* (London, 1905).

Burley, Rosa and *Caruthers, Frank L.,* 'Edward Elgar. The Record of a Friendship' (London, 1972).

Byard, Herbert, in *The Concerto* (ed. Ralph Hill, London, 1952).

Cardus, Neville, 'Elgar' in *Ten Composers* (London, 1945), and *A Composer's Eleven* (London, 1968).

Chambers, H. A., ed., 'Edward Elgar: Centenary Sketches' (London, 1957), contributors: *Sir John Barbirolli, Carice Elgar Blake, Sir Adrian Boult, H. A. Chambers, Bernard Herrmann, Alan J. Kirby, Yehudi Menuhin, Dora M. Powell, Stanford Robinson, David Willocks* and *Percy M. Young.*

Colles, H. C., Analytical Notes (*Musical Times*) on Symphony No. 1 (*December* 1908), Piano Quintet (November 1919) and Cello Concerto (February 1920).

Cox, David, 'Edward Elgar' in *The Symphony,* vol. ii (ed. Robert Simpson, London, 1967).

Cumberland, Gerald, 'Elgar' in *Set Down in Malice* (London, 1919).

Dann, Mary G., 'Elgar's Use of Sequence' (*Music and Letters,* July 1938; part of degree thesis at Rochester, U.S.A.).

Dent, Edward J., article in Adler's *Handbuch der Musikgeschichte* (1931).

Dunhill, Thomas F., 'Sir Edward Elgar' (London, 1938).

Appendix D—Bibliography

Fiske, Roger, 'The Enigma: a solution' (*Musical Times*, November 1969), a plea for 'Auld Lang Syne' as Enigma, but see below.

Fox Strangways, A. H., 'Elgar' (*Music and Letters*, April 1934).

——, letter to editor (*Music and Letters*, January 1935), rejecting 'Auld Lang Syne' as Enigma.

Gaisberg, Fred, 'Music on Record' (London, 1946).

Gorton, Canon C. V., 'Interpretation of the Librettos of the Oratorios' (the three in Chapter IX) (London, 1907).

Gray, Cecil, 'Edward Elgar' in *A Survey of Contemporary Music* (Oxford, 1924).

Grew, Sydney, 'Sir Edward Elgar, O.M.' in *Our Favourite Musicians* (London, 1924).

Hadden, J. Cuthbert, 'Modern Musicians' (London, 1913).

Howes, Frank, 'Edward Elgar' in *The Heritage of Music*, vol. iii (Oxford, 1951).

——, 'The Two Elgars' (*Music and Letters*, January 1935).

——, 'The English Renaissance' (London, 1966).

——, 'Nimrod on Strauss' (*Musical Times*, June 1970).

Hurd, Michael, 'Elgar' (London, 1969).

Jackson, Sir Barry, 'Elgar's *Spanish Lady*' (*Music and Letters*, January 1943).

Jaeger, A. J., Analytical Notes on *Gerontius* (1900), *The Apostles* (1903), *In the South* (1904) and *The Kingdom* (1906), (London).

Johnstone, Arthur, 'Musical Criticisms' (Manchester, 1905).

Jose, Everard, 'The Significance of Elgar' (London, 1934).

Keeton, A. E., 'Elgar and Quotations' (*Musical Opinion*, August 1942).

——, 'Elgar's Music for *The Starlight Express*' (*Music and Letters*, January, 1945).

Kennedy, Michael, 'Portrait of Elgar' (London, 1968).

Lambert, Herbert, 'Modern British Composers' (London, 1923).

Langford, Samuel, 'Musical Criticisms' (ed. Neville Cardus, London, 1929).

LISTENER, THE (30th July 1942), Carner, Mosco, 'Elgar as Symphonist'.

——, (4th November 1943), Hutchings, Arthur, 'Elgarian Oratorio and its Background'.

McVeagh, Diana M., 'Edward Elgar: his life and music' (London, 1955).

——, 'Elgar: an Appreciation' (Elgar Society, 1955).

——, 'Elgar's Birthplace' (*Musical Times*, June 1957).

——, 'Ashton's Enigma Ballet' (*Musical Times*, December 1968).

——, 'Elgar's Concert Allegro' (*Musical Times*, February 1969).

Appendix D—Bibliography

Maine, Basil, 'Elgar: his Life and Work' (2 vols., London, 1933).

Mason, Daniel Gregory, 'Contemporary Composers' (New York, 1918).

MONTHLY MUSICAL RECORD (March–April 1947), Wood, Ralph W., 'Enigma Derivations'.

—— (October 1948), Gregory, Robin, 'Elgar's use of nobilmente'.

Moore, Jerrold N., 'Elgar as a University Professor' (Musical Times, October and November 1960).

——, 'An Elgar Discography' (London, 1963).

——, 'Elgar. A Life in Photographs' (London, 1972).

MUSIC AND LETTERS (January 1935), contributors to special issue: Donald Tovey, Hubert Foss, Vaughan Williams, Brent Smith, Frank Howes and W. H. Reed.

—— (April 1942), Dickinson, A. E. F., 'The Drama behind Elgar's Music'.

MUSIC SURVEY (June 1951), Dickinson, A. E. F., 'The Isolation of Elgar'.

MUSICAL OPINION (April 1945), Hunt, Reginald, 'Elgar and the Common Touch'.

MUSICAL STANDARD (13th October 1900), 'Edward Elgar's Hobbies'.

MUSICAL TIMES (October 1900), biographical, portrait, analysis, etc.

—— (April 1934), contains list of articles on Elgar published in the magazine during his lifetime.

—— (January 1938), Judd, Percy, 'Elgar's Part-Songs'.

—— (July 1949), Godman, Stanley, 'The Elgars of Dover'.

—— (August 1949), Jacobs, Arthur, 'Elgar's Solo Songs'.

—— (June 1957), contributors to Centenary Number: Vaughan Williams, John Ireland, Julius Harrison, Sir Arthur Bliss, Herbert Howells, Gordon Jacob, Edmund Rubbra, Patrick Hadley, J. A. Westrup, Sir Steuart Wilson, Herbert W. Sumsion, Eric Blom, Frank Howes, Sir George Dyson, Thomas Armstrong, Sir Ernest Bullock, W. Greenhouse Allt, Edric Cundell, R. J. F. Howgill, Maurice Johnstone, Eric Warr, Alec Robertson, Diana McVeagh and Harold Rutland.

—— (March 1960), Wykes, David, 'Elgar's Cello Concerto: A Query'.

Newman, Ernest, 'Elgar' (The Music of the Masters, London, 1905).

——, 'Edward Elgar' (The Speaker, 22nd December 1901).

——, 'Elgar and his Enigma' (Sunday Times, 16th, 23rd, 30th April, 7th May, 1939).

——, 'Elgar and his "Stately Sorrow"' (The Listener, 11th March 1954).

Appendix D—Bibliography

Newman (cont.), 'The Artist and the Man' (*Sunday Times*, 13th November 1955).

——, Analytical Notes (*Musical Times*) on Violin Concerto (October 1910), Symphony No. 2 (May 1911) and *The Spirit of England* (May 1916).

PALL MALL GAZETTE (21st March 1904), 'Elgar in London'.

Parrott, Ian, 'Variation for a Dog?' (*Music Teacher*, January 1956).

——, 'Was Elgar's Orchestration Impeccable?' (*The Chesterian*, 1957).

——, 'The Enigma: A New Slant' (Elgar Society, 1968).

——, 'Elgar's Associations with Wales' (*Anglo-Welsh Review*, Summer 1969).

——, 'Elgar's Two-Fold Enigma: a Religious Sequel' (*Music and Letters*, 1973).

Porte, John F., 'Sir Edward Elgar' (London, 1921).

Powell, Richard C., 'Elgar's Enigma' (*Music and Letters*, July 1934).

Powell, Mrs Richard (Dorabella), 'Edward Elgar: Memories of a Variation' (London, 1937, 1947 and 1949).

——, 'The First Performances of *The Apostles* and *The Kingdom*' (*Musical Times*, January 1960).

Reed, W. H., 'Elgar as I knew him' (London, 1936).

——, 'Elgar' (London, 1939 and 1943).

——, 'Elgar' (*Cobbett's Cyclopaedic Survey of Chamber Music*, 1929).

——, 'Elgar's Violin Concerto' (*Music and Letters*, January 1935).

——, 'Elgar's Third Symphony' (*The Listener*, 28th August 1935).

Sams, Eric, 'Elgar's cipher letter to Dorabella' (*Musical Times*, February 1970).

——, 'Variations on a Original Theme (Enigma)' (*Musical Times*, March 1970).

——, 'Elgar's Enigma: A Past Script and a Postscript' (*Musical Times*, July 1970).

Shaw, George Bernard, 'Sir Edward Elgar' (*Music and Letters*, January 1920).

Sheldon, A. J., 'Edward Elgar' (London, 1932).

Shera, F. H., 'Elgar: Instrumental Works' (*Musical Pilgrim*, London, 1931).

Shore, Bernard, 'Elgar's Second Symphony' (*Sixteen Symphonies*, London, 1949).

Stone, Irving J., 'Edward Elgar' (*The Musical Record*, Philadelphia, 1933).

Appendix D—Bibliography

STRAND MAGAZINE (May 1904), 'Dr Elgar' (interview by Rupert de Cordova).

Streatfeild, R. A., 'Un Musicista Inglese (*Rivista d'Italia*, October, 1912).

Thompson, Herbert, Analytical Notes on *Caractacus* (London, 1898).

Tovey, Sir Donald F., Analytical Notes on *Enigma Variations, Cockaigne, In the South, Introduction and Allegro,* Violin Concerto, Symphony No. 2, *Falstaff* and Cello Concerto (*Essays in Musical Analysis,* London, 1935–9 and *Some English Symphonists,* London, 1941).

——, 'Elgar, Master of Music' (*Music and Letters,* January 1935).

Turner, E. O., 'Tempo Variations with Examples from Elgar' (*Music and Letters,* July 1938).

Vaughan Williams, Ralph, 'What have we learnt from Elgar?' (*Music and Letters,* January 1935).

Webb, Alan, 'A Curator's Notebook' (Worcester, 1969 and 1970).

Westrup, Professor Sir Jack, 'Elgar's Enigma' (*Royal Musical Association,* April 1960).

Whittall, Arnold, 'Elgar's Last Judgement' (*The Music Review,* vol. 26, No. 1, February 1965).

Wood, Sir Henry J., 'My Life of Music' (London, 1938).

WORLD, THE (11th December 1901), 'Dr Edward Elgar at Malvern'.

—— (22nd October 1912), 'Sir Edward Elgar O.M.'.

Young, Percy M., 'Elgar O.M.' (London, 1955).

——, 'Letters of Edward Elgar' (London, 1956).

——, 'Letters to Nimrod from Edward Elgar' (London, 1965).

——, 'A History of British Music', Chapter 12 (London, 1967).

——, ed., 'A Future for English Music', Birmingham University Lectures (London, 1968).

APPENDIX E

(With information compiled by Alan Webb for the Elgar Society)

1857–9   The Birthplace at Broadheath, some three miles from Worcester, stands between the Tenbury and Bromyard roads, and is signposted at both junctions. The three museum rooms are open daily (except Wednesdays), 1.30 to 6.30 p.m., or by special appointment.

            Broadheath Common, to which Elgar often returned in boyhood, was probably the place where the *Wand of Youth* music germinated.

1860–6   1 Edgar Street, Worcester (now Tower House, Severn Street). The family lived here until about 1864, removing then to new business premises at 10 High Street, almost opposite St Helen's Church (now engulfed in Messrs Russell and Dorrell's extensions).

1866–79   With his family over their music shop (10 High Street, Worcester).

1879–83   With married sister Pollie at Loretto Villa, 12 Chestnut Walk, Worcester.

1883–9   With married sister Lucy at 4 Field Terrace, Bath Road, Worcester.

1889–90   After his marriage, at 3 Marloes Road, Kensington, and Oaklands, Fountain Road, Upper Norwood.

1890–1   51 Avonmore Road, West Kensington.

1891–9   Forli, Alexandra Road, Malvern (named after Melozzo da Forli, who painted angels playing instruments). *Enigma Variations.*

1898–1903   Birchwood Lodge, Storridge, near Malvern (as a summer cottage). *The Dream of Gerontius.*

Appendix E—Houses where Elgar lived

1899–1904   Craeg Lea, Malvern Wells (the name is an anagram of C A E Elgar). *Gerontius, Cockaigne, The Apostles.*

1904–11   Plas Gwyn, Hampton Park Road, Hereford. *Introduction and Allegro, The Kingdom,* Symphony No. 1, Violin Concerto, Symphony No. 2.

1912–21   Severn House, Netherhall Gardens, Hampstead (this house no longer exists). *Falstaff, The Music Makers, The Spirit of England.*

1917–21   Brinkwells, near Fittleworth, West Sussex (as a summer cottage). Violin Sonata, String Quartet, Piano Quintet, Cello Concerto. Re-thatched in 1967.

1921–3   37 St James's Place, London.

1923–7   Napleton Grange, Kempsey, near Worcester.

1927–8   Battenhall Manor, Worcester. This house (said to have been haunted) now no longer exists.

1928–9   Tiddington House, Stratford-on-Avon (now demolished).

1929–34   Marl Bank, Rainbow Hill, Worcester. Elgar died here on 23rd February 1934. Demolished, 15th October 1969, to make room for flats.

Several of the above houses have a plaque bearing the words 'Sir Edward Elgar lived in this house', with the dates.

INDEX

INDEX

Index

Index